The Context of Legislating

The Context of Legislating provides a much-needed examination of how the rules, resources, and political conditions within and surrounding different institutions raise or lower the costs of legislating. Using data tracking over 1,100 legislators, 230 committees and 12,000 bills introduced in ten state lower chambers, Shannon Jenkins examines how political conditions and institutional rules and resources shape the arc of the legislative process by raising the costs of some types of legislative activity and lowering the costs of others. Jenkins traces these important contextual effects across the legislative process, examining bill introduction, committee processing and floor passage of bills in these legislatures. The analysis reveals that institutional variables shape the legislative process on their own, but they also have important interactive effects that shape the behavior of actors in these chambers. After tracing these effects across the legislative process, the book concludes by examining the practical implications of these analytical findings. How can the rules of institutions be designed to create effective legislatures? And what do these findings mean for those who seek to shape the policies produced by these institutions?

Understanding of how the context of legislating shapes the outputs of legislatures is a critical element of understanding legislatures that has been sorely missing. An original and timely resource for scholars and students researching state legislatures and state politics.

Shannon Jenkins is Chair and Associate Professor of Political Science at the University of Massachusetts, Dartmouth. Her research focuses on state and local politics, with a focus on decision-making in state legislatures and state and local political parties.

'Increasingly, American political scientists are recognizing the advantages of comparative study at the state level. Shannon Jenkins has produced a study that advances our knowledge of how the institutional and political context—the rules, structures and partisan arrangements—influence the making of law in our states. It is a welcome addition to the new research on state legislatures.'

Gary Moncrief, University Distinguished Professor Emeritus,
Boise State University

The Context of Legislating

Constraints on the Legislative
Process in the United States

Shannon Jenkins

Routledge
Taylor & Francis Group

NEW YORK AND LONDON

First published 2016
by Routledge
711 Third Avenue, New York, NY 10017

and by Routledge
2 Park Square, Milton Park, Abingdon, Oxon, OX14 4RN

First issued in paperback 2018

Routledge is an imprint of the Taylor & Francis Group, an informa business

Library of Congress Cataloging in Publication Data
A catalog record for this book has been requested

ISBN 13: 978-1-138-59965-9 (pbk)
ISBN 13: 978-1-138-68442-3 (hbk)

Typeset in Times New Roman
by Florence Production Ltd, Stoodleigh, Devon, UK

Contents

Illustrations

Figures

Tables

Acknowledgments

Many years ago, I was talking with John Frendreis, then my dissertation advisor, about potential dissertation topics. After having worked with him and Alan Gitelson for several years on a project about political parties, I was pretty much done with that topic at that point. Fortunately for me, John casually tossed off a comment about how the data we had collected might be used for an interesting project looking at state legislatures. Many years later, here I am still writing about state legislatures and how they work. I consider myself lucky to have found a research topic that truly interests me, and I am thankful for the guidance I received in graduate school that put me on this path. I am extremely grateful for the guidance and mentoring from John Frendreis, Alan Gitelson, John Pelissero, and others at Loyola University, where I completed my graduate work.

I have also been fortunate to land a position at the University of Massachusetts, Dartmouth; my institution and my colleagues have been incredibly supportive of my work, from research and travel support to sabbatical leaves, which has enabled me to focus on this project and see it to fruition. In particular, I'd like to thank my reference librarian, Matt Sylvain, for all the help he has provided in digging up obscure bits of data and facts that were not readily available on the Internet.

Numerous employees of these legislative chambers helped too, both in providing data and in spending time talking to me to help make sense of what I was seeing. It was good fun to talk to other people who were just as interested in the inner workings of legislatures, and their insights were extremely helpful in understanding both their chamber and the legislative process generally. These people often toil under difficult political conditions, so their willingness to share what they know was much appreciated.

It also goes without saying that state politics is one of the best subfields in political science. While my work cannot compare to the many giants in this field who have come before me, their work has inspired me. I have also been the beneficiary of helpful feedback, useful information, and supportive commiseration about the difficulty over collecting and analyzing state political data over the many years that I have worked on this project. Discussants, chairs, and audience members have provided commentary at a variety of disciplinary conferences when I presented my preliminary work on this project, but in particular, the State Politics and Policy Conference has been a book-saver for me on numerous occasions, both for supportive feedback and insightful suggestions from my state politics colleagues.

I would also like to thank all of the students who worked with me on this project. Students in my Women and Politics and State Legislatures senior seminars (Bethany Berube, Aaron Bryant, Jennifer Denker, Christopher Dinan, Gregory Dorman, Michelle Hall, Justin Lacasse, Katie Olson, Diana Robbins, Brett Schricker, Meghan Thompson, and Courtney Torres) worked diligently to collect data; in the process, they learned what political science research truly entails, for better or for worse. Numerous student workers (Max Cohen, John Cotreau, Angelica Colon, Samantha Egge, Ryan Gallagher, Chris Madeiros, Amanda Maier, Erin McDonagh, Samantha Pettey, Betsy Rivera, Michael St. Martin, and Travis Ward) also helped me finish and check the legislative process data and gather additional information.

Lastly, I'd like to thank my family for their support during my career. Unfortunately, neither Bill Jenkins nor Rich Bokor are here to appreciate the results of this project, but I know they would have been proud. I am hopeful that Ann Bokor and Judy Jenkins will be proud too. I know I would not be as successful I am today without their support.

My children, Quinlan and Berkley Roscoe, had to put up with many distracted hours from their mother as I worked on this project. As deadlines approached, they have been incredibly understanding about the times when I needed to focus on this and not them. Hopefully, they'll still turn out okay— time will tell. Thanks guys.

Finally, none of this would be possible without the support of my husband, Doug Roscoe. Our relationship is a true partnership, and words cannot express how grateful I am for the help he has given me both at home and at work. Numerous successful women have noted that the most important decision a woman can make is the partner with whom she choose to spend her life. I sure picked a winner. Thanks Doug.

1   The Context of Legislating

In the 2007–2008 legislative session, legislators in the Pennsylvania state house introduced over 2,800 bills for consideration. Across the country in Wyoming, though, legislators introduced only 506 bills. Legislators in Pennsylvania may have been overwhelmed by the volume of legislation before them as they passed only 5.6 percent of these bills, one of the lowest rates in the nation that year. Legislators from Arkansas, on the other hand, appear to have breezed through the approximately 1,800 bills introduced during the same period as they managed to enact over 57.4 percent of these proposals, one of the highest enactment rates for any legislature in the country. In one legislature, two white, male, Democratic legislators who were also committee chairs co-sponsored about the same number of bills (946 and 943), but one of these legislators served as lead sponsor on just 10 bills, while the other legislator lead sponsored 23 bills. Two female Republicans, each serving in different chambers, lead sponsored 10 bills, but one of these legislators co-sponsored 774 bills, while the other co-sponsored just 32.

What accounts for the tremendous variation in the activity levels of legislators and legislatures across the country? Do legislators in Pennsylvania simply work harder than legislators in Wyoming? Or do Pennsylvania legislators work less hard than those serving in Arkansas? Despite widespread political mistrust of politicians on the part of the American public these days, the answer to this question almost certainly is not that some legislators are lazy, while others are hard working.

Could this be driven by the fact that there are different types of people serving in these institutions then? Research suggests that this may explain some of the variation. Different types of legislators have different priorities and act differently, but the differences in who serves in many of these chambers are not all that large. For instance, much research has shown that female legislators act differently than their male counterparts (Berkman and O'Connor 1993; Cammisa and Reingold 2004; Carey et al.1998; Jewell and Whicker 1994; Saint-Germain 1989; Swers 2002), but in 2008,

22.0 percent of all Arkansas legislators were female, compared to 14.6 percent of all Pennsylvania legislators and 23.3 percent of all Wyoming legislators. There is larger variation in the percentage of minority legislators in these institutions, but in most state legislatures, the percentage of African American and other minority legislators is small, well below the 15 percent threshold that critical mass theorists identify as the threshold for potential influence (Beckwith and Cowell-Meyers 2007; Kanter 1977). So differences in the type of legislators who serve in these institutions may partially cause some of the variation in the legislative process in these institutions, but there still remains a good deal of variation that is left to explain.

Unfortunately though, little is known about how to account for variation in the inner workings of legislatures, particularly when trying to explain variation in patterns across institutions. While research in the states has looked at how the role of committees in state legislatures varies or why state legislators vote the way they do, less research has looked at the most important function of legislatures: the production of legislation. The research that does exist on the legislative process tends to focus on how the characteristics of individuals shape legislative activity. Research has examined how factors such as race, gender, and seniority shape the activity and effectiveness levels of individual legislators and as a result the workings of legislative institutions. But most of this research has examined how these factors operate in a single institution. As a result, there is a good deal of conflict in these findings. For instance, some research finds women are equally effective legislators (Jeydel and Taylor 2003; Saint-Germain 1989; Thomas 1991, 1994), while other research has found they are more effective (Volden and Wiseman 2007); still others show that the success rate of female legislators varies across institutions, but they do not really offer an explanation for this variation (Bratton and Haynie 1999).

Even those studies that move away from a focus on the characteristics of legislators tend to focus on a single institution, most commonly the U.S. House or Senate.[1] So we know a good deal about how legislating in the U.S. Congress works, but we know less about whether or not these findings transfer to other institutions. What is missing from these studies is an understanding of how the context in which these activities take place shape what happens in legislatures. As a result, there is a clear gap in our understanding of the process of legislating. Little is known how the milieu in which legislating takes place shapes the outcomes that institutions produce.

Clearly, the actions of those individuals who serve in these institutions and those who want to shape outcomes of these institutions show they believe context matters. At the beginning of each session, legislators caucus and come together to craft the rules of the institution. Legislators may pass rules that empower party leaders and limit the legislative process—or not. For example, in Georgia in 2005, Republicans passed a rule allowing the majority party leader to appoint majority party members with full voting privileges to any standing committee at any point in the legislative process (Squire 2012, 280–281). It is obvious that these legislators believed that the powers afforded to party leaders and the rules that the institutions establish influence the sorts of outputs these institutions produce.

Voters also seem to believe context matters, as can be seen with the passage of ballot initiatives focused on changing the legislative process or limiting the amount of resources available to legislators. For instance, the GAVEL (Give a Vote to Every Legislator) initiative, passed by 72 percent of Colorado voters in 1988, amended the Colorado state constitution to prevent committee chairs from pocket vetoing bills and binding caucus votes, among other provisions; passage of this amendment altered the way the legislature operated (Binder, Kogan and Kousser 2011). Measures such as this and California's 1984 Proposition 24, which changed the legislative process for selecting committee members, were proposed and sometimes passed by voters under the assumption that legislative resources and operations matter in terms of the policies produced in state legislatures. And of course, the term limits movement was predicated on the notion that changing the rules of who could serve and for how long would fundamentally alter the way these institutions worked.[2]

Parties and groups work to control these chambers for the same reason; control of the institution, they appear to believe, leads to control of the outputs of said institution. Groups wage extensive campaigns to elect like-minded legislators, and party leaders allocate resources not just as a reward for party loyalty, but also as a means to maximize the probability of retaining or regaining control of the legislature.

But despite apparent widespread beliefs about the importance of chamber arrangements and rules, the resources available to legislators, and the political conditions surrounding and within the legislature, little political science research has examined how variations in these factors shape the actions of the legislators who work within these institutions and the legislative process. Some research has examined these matters at the chamber level, but what is needed is an analysis that examines how these factors shape the workings inside these institutions, an effort that is undertaken here. How do limits on bill introductions shape the activity of legislators and the legislative process? Do the tools legislators give to party leaders matter? How do restrictions on committee activity influence the winnowing of legislation? Looking at these questions in a variety of institutional settings will help determine how variations in these settings shape the most important functions of legislature: policy outputs.

Table 1.1 State Legislation Descriptive Statistics

State	Bills Passed (%)	Sponsors Per Bill	Bills with One Sponsor (%)	Bills Sponsored by Committee (%)	Amendments Proposed Per Bill	Amendments Passed (%)
Arkansas	57.4	3.91 Avg. 135 Max. 11.75 SD	74.4	10.8%	.48 Avg. 7 Max. .815 SD	98.7
Delaware	38.0	7.03 Avg. 38 Max. 6.63 SD.	21.7	NA	.52Avg. 7 Max. .971 SD	35.5
Georgia	37.0	3.4 Avg. 6 Max. 2.04 SD	30.6	NA	UA	UA
Indiana	11.6	2.13 Avg. 12 Max. 1.32 SD	44.2	NA	.26 Avg. 15 Max. .99 SD	59.7
Ohio	15.2	10.78 Avg. 88 Max. 12.14 SD	24.1	NA	UA	UA

Oregon	30.3	3.84 Avg. 55 Max. 6.03 SD	46.6	15.7*	UA	UA
Pennsylvania	5.6	31.09 Avg. 163 Max. 19.85 SD	3.5	NA	UA	UA
Vermont	16.0	6.46 Avg. 114 Max. 11.64 SD	35.5	6.5	.19 Avg. 10 Max. .83 SD.	69.0
Wisconsin	11.0	11.27 Avg. 53 Max. 8.10 SD	5.4	5.8	.18 Avg. 8 Max. .53 SD	62.4
Wyoming	38.44	3.12 Ave. 13 Max. 2.32 SD	31.53	22.8		76.2

Note: Only House sponsors of bills were included in sponsorship calculations as some chambers allow senators to be listed as sponsors while others do not. NA = Not Applicable, Committees cannot sponsor bills in these chambers. UA = Data unavailable on state legislative website. Committee sponsored bills not included in numerator or denominator in calculating % with one sponsor. * In Oregon, an additional 14.3% of bills were introduced on behalf of individuals in the executive branch

This book analyzes this—the ways in which legislative context matters—by examining, in detail, the legislative process in ten U.S. state lower chambers in the 2007–2008 session. The data collected for this effort includes information on over 1,100 legislators, 225 committees, and 12,000 bills. Included in the dataset is information about bill sponsorships, co-sponsorships, amendment sponsorships, committee referrals, committee reports, and House passage. This data allows for a comprehensive look at the legislative process from start to finish in ten U.S. state legislatures: Arkansas, Delaware, Georgia, Indiana, Ohio, Oregon, Pennsylvania, Vermont, Wisconsin, and Wyoming.[3] While it is difficult to pick a sample that resembles all other states on key characteristics, care was taken to select states that vary on key contextual factors, but that also resemble a wide variety of legislatures in the U.S. Importantly, these chambers vary in terms of the volume of legislation they process and enact, as shown in Table 1.1. For example, Pennsylvania, on the low end, enacts less than 6 percent of all bills that are introduced, while Arkansas enacted more than 57 percent of the bills that were introduced in the 2007–2008 legislative session. On all of the measures presented here, such as bill introductions and sponsorship rates, there are fairly large differences between these chambers. Thus, there is considerable variation in the legislative process to be explained.

Next, these states also vary on a number of important political characteristics, including legislative professionalism, party control, region, the presence of term limits and the percent of female and minority legislators, as shown in Table 1.2. Three states are among the top ten most professional state legislatures (Wisconsin, Pennsylvania, and Ohio), while two states rank in the bottom ten (Indiana and Wyoming) (Squire 2007). There are at least two states from each of the census regions and an even split in terms of party control of the house. The margin of this party control varies, with slim majorities in Pennsylvania and larger majorities in states like Arkansas and Wyoming. There is divided government in states where Democrats control the house (Pennsylvania) and in states where Republicans control the house (Delaware), and there are unified Democratic states and unified Republican states. Term limits exist in two of these states, slightly less than the 30 percent of all states that have these measures. Some of these states also rank among the highest in terms of the percentage of female legislators (Vermont) and African American legislators (Georgia), while other states rank fairly low (Pennsylvania for women, and Oregon, Vermont, and Wyoming for African Americans). Clearly, there is a good deal of variation in these factors among these chambers.

In addition, these states exhibit variation on how power is dispersed in the legislature and rules governing the legislative process, as shown in Table 1.3. For instance, Indiana allocates a great deal more power to its party

Table 1.2 State Political Characteristics

State	Region	Legislative Professionalism (Rank)	Party Control	Majority Size	Divided Government	Term Limits (in years)	Female Legislators (%)	African American Legislators (%)
Arkansas	S	.104 (41)	D	75.00	No	6	22.0	11.0
Delaware	S	.151 (26)	R	53.66	Yes	None	29.3	9.1
Georgia	S	.107 (37)	R	58.89	No	None	21.1	23.9
Indiana	MW	.106 (42)	D	51.00	Yes	None	17.0	7.0
Ohio	MW	.315 (7)	R	52.53	No	8	16.2	10.1
Oregon	W	.153 (25)	D	51.67	No	None	31.7	0
Pennsylvania	NE	.339 (6)	D	50.25	Yes	None	13.3	5.9
Vermont	NE	.117 (28)	D	62.00	No	None	38.7	0
Wisconsin	MW	.459 (3)	R	51.51	Yes	None	22.2	6.1
Wyoming	W	.057 (48)	R	71.67	No	None	28.3	0

Note: Legislative Professionalism scores are from Squire (2007) for 2003. The percent of female legislators comes from the Center for American Women and Politics, and the percent of black legislators comes from the National Black Caucus of State Legislators for the 2007–2008 session

Table 1.3 Key Chamber Rules

State	Leader Tools	Committee Power	Limits on the Number of Co-Sponsors	Deadline for Adding Co-Sponsors	Limits on the Number of Bill Introductions	Deadline for Bill Introductions	Total Bill Processing Limits
Arkansas	2.00	3.0	0	0	0	0	0
Delaware	3.00	4.0	0	0	0	0	0
Georgia	3.75	5.0	0	0	0	1	1
Indiana	4.17	4.0	1	0	1	1	3
Ohio	2.50	3.0	0	0	0	0	0
Oregon	3.50	5.0	0	1	0	0	1
Pennsylvania	2.50	5.0	0	1	0	0	1
Vermont	3.50	5.0	0	1	0	1	2
Wisconsin	3.00	4.0	0	0	0	0	0
Wyoming	1.83	5.0	1	1	0	1	3

Note: Leader tools from Mooney (2010). Data on bill processing comes from NCSL (1996) and was verified through conversations with the chamber clerks

leaders than Wyoming does (Mooney 2010), despite the fact that both rank low on measures of professionalization. Several states have no limits on bill processing, while both Indiana and Wyoming have three limits on the legislative process, despite the great variation in the power allocated to party leaders (NCSL 1996).[4] There is less variation on the powers afforded to committees here, but there is at least some difference to examine here.

Thus, there is a good deal of variation in the resources, limits, and political conditions that might shape the legislative process in these chambers which allows for an examination of the way these contextual factors shape the legislative process, the focus of this book. The legislative process is traced from start to finish—from the introduction of legislation to the processing of this legislation in committee to the final step, floor passage, because the effects of these contextual factors are not consistent on all types of activities and at all stages in the process.

Chapter 2 starts by examining the existing research about the legislative process and then turns to how the context in which legislating takes place may condition the results of past research. While there has been a good deal of research on the legislative process, there is very little comparative research on how this process varies based on the setting in which it takes place.

Next, Chapter 3 examines how context influences the first step in the legislative process: the introduction of legislation. At the most fundamental level, institutions have varying rules about who can introduce legislation. For instance, in some chambers, only legislators may formally introduce legislation, as is the case with the U.S. Congress. But in other chambers, such as Oregon, a wide variety of actors can introduce legislation, including committees themselves, as well as governors, bureaucrats and even interest groups or citizens. Obviously, these rules affect who introduces legislation, which will be examined in Chapter 3. But even when we limit the scope of inquiry to bills introduced by legislators, there are a number of other rules and institutional characteristics, such as limits on the number of bill introductions and control of the chamber that may influence the types of legislators who are active in these chambers. To the extent these contextual factors shape the activity levels of different types of legislators differently (and they do), then past research has missed a critical factor that affects the legislative process.

Next, Chapter 4 looks at the middle stage of the legislative process and describes how legislative context shapes the work of committees in these institutions. Many have said that "Congress at work is Congress in committee," and the same is true of committees in state legislatures. Legislators themselves consistently rate committees as important actors in state legislatures (Francis 1989). Committees in most states are empowered to pass, alter, or kill proposals that come before them; in some states, committees also have the authority to author their own bills. Some states allow committee chairs and committees a good deal of latitude in what they may do, while committee actions and powers are much more constrained in other states. Understanding how and when committees exercise their discretion and how the context in which these committees operate affects this work is important to understanding how legislation is processed in the states.

Chapter 5 looks at how all of these factors ultimately come together to shape the fate of legislation, by looking at why some legislators are more successful in this endeavor than others and why some bills are passed while others die. Past research has tended to focus on how individual characteristics shape legislative effectiveness, but what becomes clear in a multi-state study is that the effect of these variables is conditioned by institutional setting. As a result, in order to know which bills will pass and who will be successfully in securing passage of these bills, we must also look to where these decisions take place.

Finally, Chapter 6 discusses the implications of these findings, both for developing a more general theory of legislating and for institutional design and politics generally. Across all of these chapters, the key message is that *where* legislating takes places is fundamental to understanding *how* legislating works. The legislative context shapes how legislators act, how committees work, and how institutions process legislation. Others have shown how place matters in other political settings (Dreier, Mollenkopf, and Swanstrom 2013); this analysis here demonstrates that places matters in legislatures too. Factors like limits on bill introductions, leader tools, legislative professionalism, term limits, and party control all significantly shape legislator activity and success, committee actions, and bill processing. Failure to account for context leads to an incomplete understanding of the legislative process. But thinking about context can help us not only understand how the process works, but also how to shape the process to achieve desired ends.

Notes

1 See Squire and Hamm (2005) for a description of the distribution of these studies and the issues with this distribution.

2 However, neither the claims of the proponents nor the fears of the opponents of term limits have been fully realized (Cain and Kousser 2004), although they have had some impact on the way these institutions function, as Chapter 2 describes.

3 Obviously, it would be ideal to collect data on all 50 state legislatures. However, state legislatures vary widely on where and how they report legislative data, making such an effort very difficult. As a result, this study relies on a sample of the U.S. states. Care was taken to attempt to pick a sample that was both representative of states, but that also varied across key characteristics as described

here. No sample can truly represent all the legislatures in the U.S., as context does matter, but the data gathered here provides enough variation to examine the way in which context matters, something that has been missing from past research on the legislative process.

4 These rules along with rules related to committee powers, collected in 1996 by the NCSL and ASLC, were confirmed by interviews with clerks and other legislative personnel in these chambers.

References

Beckwith, Karen and Kimberly Cowell-Meyers. 2007. "Sheer Numbers: Critical Representation Thresholds and Women's Political Representation." *Perspectives on Politics* 5 (3): 553–565.

Berkman, Michael B. and Robert E. O'Connor. 1993. "Do Women Legislators Matter? Female Legislators and State Abortion Policy." *American Politics Quarterly* 21: 102–124.

Binder, Mike, Vladimir Kogan, and Thad Kousser. 2011. "How G.A.V.E.L. Changed Party Politics in Colorado's General Assembly." In *State of Change: Colorado Politics in the Twenty-First Century,* John Straayer, Robert Duffy and Courtenay Daum (Eds.). Boulder, CO: University Press of Colorado.

Bratton, Kathleen A. and Kerry L. Haynie. 1999. "Agenda Setting and Legislative Success in State Legislatures: The Effects of Gender and Race." *Journal of Politics* 61 (3): 658–679.

Cain, Bruce E. and Thad Kousser. 2004. *Adapting to Term Limits: Recent Experiences and New Directions.* San Francisco, CA: Public Policy Institute of California.

Cammisa, Anne Marie, and Beth Reingold. 2004. "Women in State Legislatures and State Legislative Research: Beyond Sameness and Difference." *State Politics and Policy Quarterly* 4: 181–210.

Carey, John M., Richard G. Niemi, and Lynda W. Powell. 1998. "Are Women State Legislators Different?" In *Women and Elective Office: Past, Present, and Future,* Sue Thomas and Clyde Wilcox (Eds.). New York: Oxford University Press.

Dreier, Peter, John Mollenkopf, and Todd Swanstrom. 2013. *Place Matters: Metropolitics for the 21st Century, 2nd edition.* Lawrence, KS: University of Kansas Press.

Francis, Wayne L. 1989. *The Legislative Committee Game: A Comparative Analysis of 50 States.* Columbus, OH: Ohio State University Press.

Jewell, Malcolm E. and Marcia L. Whicker. 1994. *Legislative Leadership in the American States.* Ann Arbor, MI: University of Michigan Press.

Jeydel, Alana and Andrew J. Taylor. 2003. "Are Women Legislators Less Effective? Evidence from the U.S. House in the 103rd–105th Congress." *Political Research Quarterly* 56: 19–27.

Kanter, Rosabeth M. 1977. "Some Effects of Proportions on Group Life: Skewed Sex Ratios and Responses to Token Women." *American Journal of Sociology* 82 (5): 965–990.

Mooney, Christopher Z. 2010. "Principals, Agents, Tools and Influence: The Dynamic of Disappointment in Legislative Leadership Influence." Paper Presented at the 2010 American Political Science Association Annual Meeting, Washington, DC.

National Conference of State Legislatures (NCSL). 1996. Accessed at www.ncsl.org/documents/legismgt/ILP/96Tab3Pt1.pdf on October 23, 2015.

Saint-Germain, Michelle. 1989. "Does Their Difference Make a Difference?: The Impact of Women on Public Policy in the Arizona State Legislature." *Social Science Quarterly* 70: 956–969.

Squire, Peverill. 2007. "Measuring Legislative Professionalism: The Squire Index Revisited." *State Politics and Policy Quarterly* 7: 211–227.

——. 2012. *The Evolution of American Legislatures: Colonies, Territories, and States, 1619–2009.* Ann Arbor, MI: University of Michigan Press.

Squire, Peverill and Keith E. Hamm. 2005. *101 Chambers: Congress, State Legislatures, and the Future of Legislative Studies.* Columbus, OH: Ohio State University Press.

Swers, Michelle. 2002. *The Difference Women Make: The Policy Impact of Women in Congress.* Chicago, IL: University of Chicago Press.

Thomas, Sue. 1991. "The Impact of Women on State Legislative Politics." *Journal of Politics* 53: 958–976.

——. 1994. *How Women Legislate.* New York: Oxford University Press.

Volden, Craig and Alan E. Wiseman. 2007. "Legislative Effectiveness in Congress." Paper Presented at the 2007 Annual Meeting of the American Political Science Association, Chicago, IL.

2 Why Context Matters

In 1998, Colorado voters passed ballot initiative 3004, commonly referred to as the GAVEL amendment—Give a Vote to Every Legislator.[1] The text of the initiative asked voters:

> Shall there be an amendment to the Colorado Constitution to require that every measure referred to a committee of reference of the General Assembly be considered by the committee upon its merits, to provide that each measure reported by a committee of reference to the Senate or House shall appear on the calendar of that chamber in the order which it was reported, and to prohibit members of the General Assembly from committing themselves or other members in a party caucus to vote in favor of or against any matter pending or to be introduced in the General Assembly?

This measure was backed by 72 percent of Colorado voters, who in one fell swoop significantly altered the way that the Colorado legislature operated. Party leaders were stripped of their ability to hold party members to caucus votes and to alter the floor calendar to punish those who failed to toe the party line. Committee chairs could no longer pocket bills, reducing their political capital in the legislature. These changes fundamentally altered who was active and who was successful in the Colorado state legislature, as Binder, Kogan and Kousser (2011) demonstrate. The changes empowered moderate legislators who began to form cross-party coalitions. Party leaders, who used to exercise substantial control over the legislative process, were stripped of their most significant powers. In essence, the rules of the game changed, and in response, the players of the game adapted in new and interesting ways. Colorado political activists and voters hoped this would happen, when they proposed and voted for the GAVEL amendment. And ultimately, the initiative was successful in opening the Colorado legislature up to a broader range of legislative proposals (Binder, Kogan and Kousser 2011).

In other words, GAVEL was successful in opening the legislature to different voices and different proposals, which is what voters seemingly wanted.

Ultimately, people vote for elected representatives with the expectation that they will produce public policies that reflect their desires. Indeed, the GAVEL initiative sprang from a sense of frustration at the lack of legislative responsiveness in Colorado. But while legislating is perhaps the most the critical job of the legislature, legislators vary in their willingness to introduce policy and in their ability to see those proposals through the legislative process. Much of this variation is due to the fact that sponsoring bills and working to ensure their passage are costly activities. Time and effort must be spent crafting legislation, convincing others to sign on, as well as shepherding proposals through committees and floor consideration. As Schiller (1995) argues, legislators are calculating individuals who consider the costs and benefits of their actions; legislators incur three types of costs when legislating: resource, opportunity, and political. Legislators have limited resources, like time, so they must consider how many resources to devote to legislating. Resources devoted to working on one bill means that resources cannot be spent on other bills or types of activities, an opportunity cost that legislators need to consider. And of course, introducing and passing legislation that alters the status quo is sure to disrupt certain interests, which may incur political costs for sponsors. Legislators will legislate when the expected benefits outweigh the costs, but will sit on the side-lines when the perceived costs outweigh the benefits (Schiller 1995, 191).

Research examining legislative activity generally focuses on understanding why some legislators are more likely to pay these costs. Studies have demonstrated that part of this variability is due to the characteristics and activities of legislators themselves. For instance, studies have examined how the number of bills a legislator sponsors the influence of passage of these bills, with some finding that more activity leads to greater economies of scale and more success (Anderson et al. 2003) and others finding less activity leads to greater success as legislators can devote more of their limited resources to ensuring each bill passes (Franzitch 1979). Institutional arrangements may also alter the nature of costs and benefits in a legislature. The effects of the GAVEL amendment demonstrate that this is clearly the other critical part of the equation in understanding legislating. For example, majority party status confers benefits on the majority party that makes it easier for members of this party to secure passage of legislation. Conversely, divided government may raise the costs of legislating, as legislators must work across the aisle to ensure successful passage of their proposals. However, very little research has examined how institutional features change the cost benefit calculus for legislators and other actors, such as committees, within these chambers, even though they surely do.

Much of the research that attempts to understand this interaction has been generated at the Congressional level, which is problematic for several reasons. First, Congress is an institution where many bills are introduced, but few are enacted into law. So for example, many have argued that representatives strategically introduce legislation; members know it is an uphill battle to secure passage of legislation, so they introduce bills to claim credit or to signal to other lawmakers. As Stewart (2001, 338) notes:

> Many members of Congress introduce bills they know will never see the light of day. This can be because members either wish to be seen as policy innovators or to use the bill introduction process as a low-cost method of demonstrating that they are on top of popular issues.

While this conventional wisdom may be true in an institution where the bill passage rate typically hovers around 5 percent of all bills introduced, it is less clear if these findings hold true at the state level where enactment rates vary considerably. For instance in 2006, enactment rates ranged from a low of approximately 3.6 percent of the 3,139 bills introduced in the Minnesota state legislature to a high of over 73 percent of the 3,176 bills introduced in the Arkansas state legislature (Rosenthal 2008, 308).

Furthermore, this focus on Congress is problematic as many factors that may change the cost/benefit calculus of actors within Congress, such as term limits or the powers of party leaders, do not vary or change slowly over time. Lack of variation precludes any analysis of the impact of some features of these institutions, while the vast differences in political time periods makes it difficult to study features of institutions that change only rarely and calls into question the generalizability of findings.

Some studies have examined the legislative process in the states by looking at the outputs of these institutions as a whole (Bowling and Ferguson 2001; Gray and Lowery 1995; Hicks and Smith 2009; Squire 1998), but few studies examine how actors in legislatures are influenced by institutional characteristics. Some research examines certain aspects of legislating (such as sponsorship or effectiveness) in multiple legislatures, but no research examines the impact of contextual factors across the legislative process, from bill introduction to committee processing to final passage.

As a result, numerous questions about our understanding of the legislative process persist. Why do introduction and enactment rates vary across legislative institutions? Credit claiming and position taking may be the norm in institutions with low enactment rates, but this may not be the case in institutions with enactment rates greater than 50 percent, which describes close to 20 percent (nine) of all state legislatures. Are the factors that influence legislative productivity and effectiveness the same across the states? While higher sponsorship rates have been found to relate to legislative effectiveness in Congress, where bill sponsorship is unlimited, in some institutions, legislators are limited in the number of bills they may introduce, suggesting this relationship may only hold in some settings. How do institutional characteristics affect the work of committees?

Committees are vital players in the legislative process, but it is not clear how institutional design affects their work. Does the ability to pocket bills enhance the role of committee in the legislative process? Are legislators more deferential to committees that have these powers? Do different types of committees, such as Appropriations or Rules Committees, kill bills at higher rates than other committees across institutions? They may in some chambers, but this may not be true in other chambers where rules restrict the ability of committees to do this. Are different types of legislators more successful in certain types of environments? Some research has found that women are more effective lawmakers in Congress. Are they more effective in all legislatures? If not, what are the features of legislatures that are conducive to the success of female legislators? Answers to these sorts of questions are critical to developing more universal theories of legislating. As Squire and Hamm (2005, 3) argue, "truly generalizable theories should be portable from one American legislature to another."

In order to begin this work of developing more generalizable theories of legislating, this chapter starts with an examination of what is known about the legislative process in U.S. legislatures as much research has examined the question of why legislators engage in the costly activity of legislating, the role of committees in the legislative process, and which legislators are more likely to be successful. Next, the second half of the chapter examines how these findings may be conditioned or alternatively clarified by context as there are a number of contextual factors that may raise or lower the cost of legislating or that change the cost-benefit calculus for actors within these institutions.

Initiating Legislation

Generally speaking, the factors that induce greater legislative activity tend to be grouped into two main categories: institutional and individual (Ellickson 1992); these factors also are related to legislative effectiveness, an issue addressed later in this chapter. The key determinants of legislative activity in the institutional category are majority party status and leadership status.[2] Both of these factors provide benefits to legislators that reduce the costs of legislating; as a result, these legislators tend to be more active as sponsors of bills, but less active as co-sponsors, as they have less need for the capital that comes from signing others' bills. So for example, research has confirmed that members of the majority party in Congress are more active sponsors of legislation (Frantzich 1979; Garand and Burke 2006; Platt 2008), but majority party membership is negatively related to co-sponsorship levels (Garand and Burke 2006; Koger 2003). Given that the two major parties compete vigorously for control of legislative chambers, the divergent effects of majority party status on legislative activity is not altogether surprising. Parties seek to control legislatures under the assumption that the majority party control provides benefits that make it more likely to secure passage of their policy initiatives. If majority party members are more likely to pass bills, then this should induce them to put more initiatives forward. But minority party members, who lack these benefits, are less likely to win, so they may be more inclined to sign on to other proposals in the hopes of earning similar support for their own proposals.

Over and above any benefit stemming from majority party status, legislators who hold positions of leadership, including party leader and committee chair positions, are also more likely to be active (Frantzich 1979; Garand and Burke 2006; Hamm, Harmel and Thompson 1983; Platt 2008; Schiller 1995). This is due to the fact that assuming positions of leadership leads to the acquisition of institutional resources that party leaders can use to their own personal advantage; as with majority party members, the logic is then that legislators will more actively introduce legislation because they are more likely to succeed. However, leadership is negatively associated with co-sponsorship, as less powerful and advantaged legislators seem to be more likely to engage in co-sponsorship (Bratton and Rouse 2011; Volden and Wiseman 2007). Time devoted to leading the chamber has to come from somewhere—that somewhere appears to be co-sponsoring legislation.

Next, characteristics of individual legislators, such as gender, seniority, and race, have been found to influence legislative activity, but these findings are not always consistent. For example, research shows clear differences in the type of bills that female legislators introduce, with female legislators being more likely to focus on bills related to so called women's issues (Bratton and Haynie 1999; Reingold 2000; Swers 2002; Thomas 1994). But some research shows female legislators' activity levels are no different from their male counterparts in Congress (Platt 2008) and some state legislatures (Reingold 2000), while other research shows them to be more active both as sponsors and co-sponsors (Rocca and Sanchez 2008). Black legislators have been found to sponsor and co-sponsor fewer bills in Congress (Garand and Burke 2006; Rocca and Sanchez 2008), although some research has found higher levels of co-sponsorship for black legislators in Congress (Volden and Wiseman 2007) and in some state legislatures (Bratton and Rouse 2011).

Seniority is also related to activity, with more senior legislators sponsoring more legislation (Platt 2008). The effects of seniority on co-sponsorship are less clear, though, as some find seniority is negatively related to co-sponsorship activity, with more senior legislators co-sponsoring less frequently than their more junior counterparts (Garand and Burke 2006; Rocca and Sanchez 2008; Wilson and Young 1997), while others find increased levels of co-sponsorship among more senior legislators (Krehbiel 1995). On the one hand, time spent in legislatures building networks may make co-sponsorship less costly, but on the other hand, if seniority leads to increased lead sponsorship, these senior legislators may have less time to dedicate to co-sponsorship.

Clearly then, individual characteristics shape who initiates legislation and influence patterns of legislating. Those legislators who are more privileged in terms of institutional positions, seniority and job security and in-group status tend to be more active sponsors because these resources make lead sponsorship less costly and therefore more attractive, while those who are less privileged are more likely to turn to co-sponsorship. Of course, these findings are not always consistent, which raises the question of why they are not, but clearly, some types of legislators are more willing and able to pay the costs associated with legislating.

Committee Processing

In legislatures in the U.S., once legislation is introduced, it is assigned to a committee for processing. Committees are an essential part of the legislative process. As with Congress, committees are important actors in U.S. state legislatures. The famous saying that Congress in committee is Congress at work could also be applied to most U.S. state legislatures (Francis and Riddlesperger 1982). As Francis (1989) found, committees are thought to be an important decision-making centers in 81 of 99 state legislative chambers and were ranked as unimportant in only three states.

Research often works from the assumption that different types of committees will play different roles in the legislative process. For example, prestige committees, such as Appropriations and Rules committees, have been assumed to play a more outsized role in the legislative process, which is why positions on these committees are coveted. Bills that are passed out of these committee are assumed to be more likely to pass; for example, Squire and Moncrief (2010, 165) note that budget bills in state legislatures are must pass bills, so committees processing budgets may ultimately be more successful in securing passing for their legislation. These committees may also serve as a locus of control over the legislative process; Binder, Kogan and Kousser (2011) found that passage of the GAVEL amendment in Colorado shifted the focus of killing power from the Rules Committee, which was dissolved by GAVEL, to the Appropriations Committee in the Colorado House. These assumptions have clear implications for report rates, and the ultimate fate of bills in the parent chamber, although these implications have not been thoroughly tested. Furthermore, there has been little research that tests whether the roles committee play vary across and within institutions or how institutional features shape the role that committees play.

Despite this lack of research, there is reason to expect that committees vary in how active they are in passing legislation out of committee and even sponsoring bills themselves. For instance, Deering (1982) found that subcommittee chairs have become more active in managing bills in Congress, but he also finds variation in both the rate at which bills are managed by committee chairs, and the rate at which committees engage in bill management and hand over management of bills to these sub-committee chairs.

But while political science research works from the assumption that committees are important agents in the legislative process (Maltzman 1997; Martorano 2006), the exact role of these committees has been up for debate. Distributive, informational and partisan theories of committee work have focused on the role committees play in legislatures generally, and tests of these theories of committee agency have commonly focused on explaining the variation in the composition and power of committees in state legis- latures, with a particular focus on the presence and prevalence of outlier committees (Battista 2004, 2006a, 2006b, 2009; Hamm, Hedlund and Martorano 2006; Hedlund and Hamm 1996; Martorano 2006; Overby and Kazee 2000; Overby, Kazee, and Prince 2004; Prince and Overby 2005; Richman 2008). Several studies have begun to move beyond such questions, looking at issues such as when and under what circumstances legislative institutions will choose different committee arrangements (Battista 2009; Martorano 2006; Richman 2008). Battista (2006a) demonstrated the utility of delving further into committee behavior; his analysis of the voting unanimity in committee votes showed that different committees in single legislature can act in ways that are consistent with a variety of roles. Having established variation in committee roles within and across institutions, the question that then arises is what factors induce committees to take on different roles and operate differently. Some of this variation may be explained by variation in the role of individual committee chairs (Deering 1982), but surely institutional rules, resources and political conditions play a role here too.

Some studies have examined the role of committees in state legislatures generally (Francis 1989; Rosenthal 1973; Van Der Silk and Redfield 1986). For instance, Van Der Silk and Redfield (1986) reported that during 1960s, committees in the Illinois house reported over 81 percent of bills, but by early 1980s, this had declined to 46 percent. But an examination of only one state makes it difficult to isolate the causes of this variation in committee activity. And there is reason to believe that resources available to committees, such as the powers afforded to them or the staff associated with increased legislative professionalism, matter; resources can help lower the costs of committee activity and empower them as agents in the legislative process. This variation in the activity level of committees may also have important implications for information, distributive, and partisan theories of committee activity. For example, if chamber rules require committees to report on all bills, as the GAVEL amendment did, partisan committees may be less effective gate-keepers of the party interest, as happened in Colorado (Binder, Kogan, and Kousser 2011). The ability to author bills may empower distributive committees as they seek to dole out benefits. Thus, the rules, resources, and political conditions in an institution may raise or lower the costs of committee action, just as they may influence the actions of legislators in a chamber. Given that nearly all legislation in U.S. state legislatures must pass through committees, understanding the role of committees in the legislative process and how this work is influenced by the institutional context in which committees reside is critical.

Passing Legislation

Ultimately, government and legislatures exist to produce policies, so after legislation is initiated and then processed through committees, the critical question is what happens next. While understanding the legislative process appears straightforward, (see any basic Introduction to American Government textbook, for example), the truth of the matter is that it is far more complex than it may seem at first glance, and what we think we know about the legislative process is not necessarily true. Krutz (2005, 315) identifies a variety of myths surrounding the legislative winnowing process and finds none of these myths are proven to be true. Thus, understanding what happens to legislation requires a nuanced look at the factors that shape the legislative process. Generally speaking, research has examined this question in three key ways: by looking at the effectiveness of individual legislators, by looking at variation in the outputs of legislative institutions, or by looking at the fate of individual bills. The first studies tend to look how individual characteristics shape legislative success, while the second type tends to look at institutional features. As a result, they miss opportunities to examine the cross-level interaction of individual and institutional effects on effective legislating.[3] Studies using bill level analysis tend to be more rare and commonly focus on one institution, again missing the potential for examining the effect of cross-institutional variation, leaving many important unanswered questions. For instance, how does party (Democratic or Republican) control shape the success of female and minority legislators? Do term limits, which truncate seniority in legislatures, undermine or enhance the effect of seniority on legislative effectiveness? Are legislatures where committees have more powers more or less deferential to the recommendations of these bodies?

Despite these limitations, there is some degree of consistency in these studies, so existing research can point to some factors that influence legislative success and bill passage. These factors are very similar to the factors that influence initiating legislation and can be grouped into the same two categories: institutional and individual. Both can provide benefits to legislators that help reduce the cost of legislating, leading to greater legislative success. As with initiating legislation, individuals who acquire institutional positions, such as committee chairs, leadership positions, or even majority party status, have access to the sorts of benefits that lead to greater success. For example, research looking at individual legislators has confirmed that members of Congress in the majority party are more successful in securing passage of legislation they sponsor (Anderson et al. 2003; Cox and Terry 2008; Frantzich 1979). Looking at the fate of individual bills, Krutz (2005) confirms this as he finds that bills sponsored by majority party members are more likely to continue on in the legislative process. The few studies that look at effectiveness at the state level also confirm that majority party status are positively related to legislative effectiveness, although the findings they present raise interesting questions about these relationships (Bratton and Haynie 1999; Ellickson 1992; Hamm, Harmel and Thompson 1983; Kirkland 2011; Miquel and Snyder 2006). For example, Miquel and Snyder (2006), who examine the North Carolina House, wonder if majority party status may have an even larger effect in other states given that North Carolina is not a particularly strong party state.

Over and above any benefit stemming from majority party status, legislators who hold positions of leadership, including party leader and committee chair positions, are also more likely to be successful (Cox and Terry 2008; Frantzich 1979; Hasecke and Mycoff 2007; Kirkland 2011). This is due to the fact that assuming positions of leadership leads to the acquisition of institutional resources that party leaders can use to move their bills forward.

Again, Miquel and Snyder (2006) raise interesting questions about the consistency of these findings across institutional settings, as they note not all party leaders control committee assignments and bill referral in the states. Third, the personal characteristics and activities of individual legislators have been found to influence legislative effectiveness. For example, one of the most consistent findings in studies of legislative effectiveness is that more senior legislators tend to be more effective legislators (Cox and Terry 2008; Ellickson 1992; Frantzich 1979; Hamm, Harmel and Thompson 1983; Kirkland 2011; Miquel and Snyder 2008). Krutz (2005) finds that the seniority of sponsors is one of the important cues surrounding a bill that determine which bills gain further consideration. Miquel and Snyder (2006) call this learning by doing and find there are no diminishing returns to the benefits of seniority.

Next, some research has shown that women are equally likely to achieve passage of the bills they introduce, after taking into account factors likely seniority, preferences and institutional position (Jeydel and Tayler 2003; Saint-Germain 1989; Thomas 1991, 1994) although Volden and Wiseman (2007; see also Volden, Wiseman, and Wittmer 2013) find women are more effective legislators. Furthermore, Bratton and Haynie (1999) find that there is some state variation in success rates, with women in Maryland being less likely and women in California being more likely to achieve passage of their bills. However, race has been found to have a consistently negative effect on effectiveness (Bratton and Haynie 1999; Ellickson 1982).

The level and type of activities legislators engage in can affect their success rates too. Anderson et al. (2003) and Cox and Terry (2008) find greater levels of activity leads to more success, although the former argue that past a certain point, the returns on activity diminish and actually grow negative. Indeed, for any given bill, multiple sponsorship is a cue that increases the likelihood of passage, suggesting a positive relationship between activity and success (Boehmer et al. 1985; Browne 1985; Kirkland 2011; Krehbiel 1995; Wilson and Young 1997).

Thus, there is some consistency in the research examining the activity of individual legislators, although there is also some degree of discrepancy, as Table 2.1 shows.

Moving beyond looking at activity and success of individual legislators, research on the role of committees, deference to their actions, and the ultimate fate of these bills is less common, despite the central role these bodies play in the legislative process. Understanding the legislative process requires examining these actors in multiple institutional settings, which may help clarify conflicting results. Institutional arrangements and conditions are designed with idea that there will be some impact on the actions of those within the institution, and the story of the GAVEL amendment clearly

Table 2.1 Summary of Research Findings on Legislative Activity and
Effectiveness

	Sponsorship	*Co-Sponsorship*	*Effectiveness*
Majority Party	+	-	+
Leadership	+	-	+
Seniority	+	M	+
Gender	M	M	M
Race	-	M	-
Activity			+

Note: Entries in cells represent the predicted relationship. M = research findings are mixed.
ND = research finds no difference. UK = research findings unknown

demonstrates that they do have some effect. So, how might these institutional arrangements and conditions shape the activities of actors in these institutions?

Legislative Context

While political science can talk with some degree of certainty about how the legislative process works and influences policy in Congress or in some state legislatures in specific areas like bill sponsorship, there is very little cross-institutional research about the legislative process at the state level (Squire and Hamm 2005). The research that does examine these questions in comparative settings tends to be limited to specific issue areas (Barnello and Bratton 2007; Boehmer et al. 2008; Bratton and Haynie 1999) or examines this question at the state institutional level (Bowling and Ferguson 2001; Gray and Lowery 1995; Hicks and Smith 2009; Squire 1998), which leaves numerous questions about the nature of legislative activity in different settings. Increasingly, political scientists are recognizing the importance of studying context as a few recent studies have looked at how contextual variables affect things like party roll rates (Anzia and Jackman 2013; Jackman 2014) and support for conference committee reports (Ryan 2014). Importantly though, these studies have not examined the effect of context across the legislative process; context may affect different types of legislative activity in different ways, as research that shows party leaders tend to be more active lead sponsors but less active co-sponsors demonstrates.

This is problematic as Squire and Hamm (2005, 126) note, "an exclusive focus on a single institution raises the possibility that theory is tailored to fit narrow circumstances." For example, Krutz (2005) finds that cues such as the partisanship of the lead sponsor and the number of sponsors play a strong role in determining how far a bill advances in the legislative process.

This may be true in an institution where only 5.2 percent of bills were enacted into law in the 1997–1998 session, but it is unclear whether or not this is true in state like Arkansas where 73 percent of all bills introduced were enacted (Rosenthal 2008, 308). In states like Arkansas, it is not clear if acquiring more sponsors is necessary to move proposals forward when the majority of proposals move forward anyway. It could be that legislators in these institutions are all active and effective, or it could be that co-sponsorship levels are unrelated to bill progress and legislative effectiveness in these chambers.

Furthermore, there is strong reason to believe that the context in which these decisions take place matters. As noted in Chapter 1, individuals and organizations compete for control of institutions and impose restrictions on their operation because they believe these things matter. In discussing legislative committees, Eulau and McCluggage (1984, 198) note that the common environment in the legislature impinges on their actions—the same is true for the actions of individual legislators. And if the common environment in one institution influences the process within it, then surely different environments will affect the legislative process in different ways. For instance, the NCSL (1996, 3–1) notes that limits on bill introductions, which are present in only some legislatures, serve to streamline the legislative process in the hopes of producing fewer introductions. In such conditions, legislators will obviously be less active, but they may also be more successful as they have more time to focus on these limited bills. Proponents of term limits argued for their passage with the assumption that they would change the way legislatures work, and while these limits have not necessarily fulfilled the greatest wishes of their supporters or the greatest concerns of their opponents, they have clearly altered the legislative process (Cain and Kousser 2004). These limits affect both individual legislators and committees. Thus, these institutional rules and arrangements raise or lower the costs of legislating and have consequences for how legislation is processed in these institutions.

These institutional variables seem to fall into two general categories: those related the political parties and partisan control of the levers of government and those related to institutional rules and resources. Of course, the former is clearly related to the latter: partisan control over legislatures bestows upon the majority party the ability to set most institutional rules. But not all rules are subject to party control. For instance, as the GAVEL examples demonstrates, voters in some states have passed constitutional amendments restricting the legislature's ability to change their own rules and regulations. Furthermore, there is some inertia in these rules, despite changes in party control. For example of the ten states examined here, as of 2015, only two states (Arkansas and Oregon) have changed legislative processing rules

collected by the National Conference of State Legislatures and the American Society of Legislative Clerks in 1996.[4] So party control of legislatures is important, but it is not the only feature of the legislative context that matters. Rules and resources matter too.

Overall, these variables serve to alter the cost-benefit calculus that comes with legislating for a variety of actors in any given legislature. In general, these political conditions and institutional arrangements will raise or lower the costs of legislating. For instance, term limits reduce the resources available to legislators, that is time and experience in the institution. As such, they may reduce the overall activity and effectiveness levels of all members of a given chamber. However, conditions and arrangements may also have different effects for different legislators. Party control should affect majority party members differently than minority party members, as the benefits of controlling the chamber accrue to the former but not the latter. Party leader powers should affect party leaders differently than rank and file members. This is why it is important to consider these how these contextual variables affect the process directly, but also through the actions of certain types of legislators.[5]

Party Related

Political parties compete for control of legislatures because they believe that to the victors go the spoils. And when they gain control of these institutions, they often act in a manner that reflects this belief. For instance, after Republicans gained control of the Illinois House in 1995, they pushed through a series of rules changes that centralized power in the hands of party leaders (Jenkins 2008, 256). Party leaders will sometimes stack committees and send important bills to these committees (Hedlund and Hamm 1996; Jewell 1962). Indeed, for Jewell (1986, as cited in Hedlund and Hamm 1996), the key to party control of the legislature was the extent to which parties controlled committees. These efforts generally bear fruit as research shows that legislators are more inclined to toe the party line when party leaders have more of these powers (Jenkins 2008, 256).

Fundamental to any party gaining access to these levers of power, then, is the attainment of majority status in these chambers. Doing so will change the cost benefit calculus for individual members of the legislature, typically to the advantage of those legislators in the majority and to the detriment of those not in the majority. Majority party members may shift to focusing on lead sponsoring bills, as they may expect to be more successful here, while minority party members may shift to focus on co-sponsoring bills, as they expect reduced effectiveness for their own bills.

Of course, in the two party system in the U.S., almost every legislature has a majority (ties are rare in state legislations), so who has that majority may matter as well. Historically, the Democratic Party has been seen as more hospitable to the concerns of both black people and women, so it is reasonable to expect that these types of legislators will be more active and effective in institutions controlled by the Democratic Party. Past research has shown this relationship is nuanced (Osborn 2003; Rocca and Sanchez 2008). Rocca and Sanchez (2008) find female legislators engage in higher levels of sponsorship and co-sponsorship under Republican control of Congress, but act no differently than their male counterparts under Democratic control of Congress. However, they find a different effect for minorities under Republican control of Congress as they are less likely to sponsor and co-sponsor bills; as with women, there is no difference under Democratic control.

So, who controls the chamber is important. However, there are at least two others aspects of partisan control of the legislature and state government that are also important. First, the margin by which the majority party controls the chamber may influence the legislative process; majority size should have its primary effect through majority party status. That is, the size of the majority party should not influence all legislators equally, although there are alternative hypothesis here. First, majority party members may be more active and more effective when the size of their majority is larger. In such conditions, it may be easier to garner a winning coalition as there are more co-partisans from whom to secure votes; as a result, passage may be more easily secured, and majority party legislators may be more active, particularly in lead sponsoring bills. In other words, large majorities decrease the costs of legislating as there is a larger pool of potential support to work with, decreasing the costs of activity and increasing the chance of success, particularly the latter.

Alternatively, Crain and Tollison (1982) demonstrate that as majority size increases, the average production of legislation decreases in state legislatures, a free riding effect confirmed by Rogers (2002). This may be due to the fact that as a group's collective action problems increase (i.e. when the party only controls the legislature by a slim margin), party members are more likely to empower leaders than in situations where their collective action problems are smaller (i.e. when the party controls the legislature by a large margin), as Mooney (2010) demonstrates in Illinois. Looking at one chamber, though, makes it difficult to disentangle the effects of majority size and leader power. Is the increase in effectiveness due to majority size or empowering party leaders?

Clearly then, party control of a chamber may condition the legislative process within that chamber, but partisan control of other parts of government will also surely alter the process within the chamber as the preferences of those outside the chamber must be taken into consideration. Indeed, studies of congressional party voting have shown that party control is also enhanced by unified control of government (Brady, Cooper, and Hurley 1979; Coleman 1999; Sinclair 1977). When one party controls both chambers of the legislature and the governor's office, then the effects of majority party status will presumably be greatest. With some degree of confidence that their legislative proposals will be successful, majority party legislators may be more active and successful. Co-sponsorship may decline among these party members as they have less need to work across party aisles. However, minority party members may be more likely to cosponsor under unified government as the need to build bridges across the aisle increases (Bratton and Rouse 2011; Kirkland 2011).

There is some debate about how divided government will impact the legislative process though. Some scholars find divided government has a negative impact on the overall legislative productivity of legislatures (Binder 2003; Coleman and Parker 1999; Gray and Lowery 1995; Kousser 2010), while others find no impact (Hicks and Smith 2009; Krehbiel 1996; Mayhew 2002). What is missing from examinations of institutional outputs is a nuanced understanding of how divided government influences the legislative process as it may produce mixed effects on patterns of legislative activity. Legislators may be less inclined to lead sponsor bills as accomplishing legislative goals may be more difficult under divided government. Conversely, co-sponsorship may become more important as a signal that a bill has broad support, leading to increased co-sponsorship activity. Divided government may also lead to less success generally, as it is harder to pass legislation when multiple branches of government are under control of different parties. Unified control of government leads to greater party unity, while divided party control leads to less party unity, presumably making it more difficult for legislators to secure passage of legislation (Jenkins 2008).

Furthermore, the impact of divided government on the legislative process may be interactive as the effect of majority party status may be muted under conditions of divided government as well. When one party controls the institutions of government, then majority party status may lead to both more activity and effectiveness. But when divided government exists, fewer benefits may accrue from majority party status, leading these legislators to be less active and have less success. Thus, divided government should directly affect legislative activity, but its effect should be greatest on majority party members.

Institution Related—Rules and Resources

When parties seek control legislatures, it is with the assumption that the ability to control and set institutional rules matter. Some of these rules, like the power of party leaders, are theoretically set by members of the entire institution—although in reality the majority party caucus typically decides these rules. Despite having this power, parties are often restrained by state constitutions, past practice, and norms in a given institution. For example, legislators in New Hampshire might desire to be paid more than $200 per session, but changing this would require a constitutional amendment, which would need to be approved by the voters. The Massachusetts legislature has a tradition of using joint committees to process legislation. Even though these joint committees serve to disadvantage the state Senate (because the House appoints more members to each committee as it is a larger body), tradition has kept them alive.[6] And despite what legislators themselves may think about how much time is needed to do their job, many state constitutions establish limits on the number of days in session; some even limit legislatures to sessions every other year.

These resources and rules are important in their own right then, independent of party control, in shaping the legislative process. Variations in these arrangements can lower the costs of action, by providing more resources to actors within the institution, or they can raise the costs of action, by erecting barriers that must be overcome. Furthermore, these costs and benefits may not be spread equally across the institution, with some actors gaining and other losing.

Legislative Professionalism

Institutions vary great in the resources they provide to those who serve in them. Some legislatures provide compensation to make serving a decent full-time job, while those serving in other institutions must clearly have other means for support. As mentioned above, New Hampshire legislators make just $200 per session with no per diem, as compared to legislators in California who make over $95,000 per year in addition to over $140 per diem for every day they are in session.[7] Additionally, there is a good deal of variation in the amount of staff provided to legislators and committees in these states. California had over 2,000 permanent staff in 2012 with 120 state legislators, while New Hampshire had only 147, despite having 424 members serving in the state legislature. It is not hard to imagine that having more money, staff, and time makes it easier to pay the costs associated with legislating.

However, research examining the effects of legislative professionalism on legislatures has been mixed. More professional legislatures attract more ambitious politicians, which makes them more responsive to their constituents (Maestas 2000). As Clucas (2003, 404) notes, this theoretical connection between professionalism and member behavior has implications for other aspects of the legislative process too as more ambitious legislators may be more active, reflecting a desire to not only be responsive to their constituents, but to also gain power and prestige within an institution. As such, with more time and resources available to legislators, it can be hypothesized that legislators will be more active under these conditions.

Legislative professionalism may have a particular impact on co-sponsorship; legislators with more time, staff and resources to devote to legislating may be able to focus more on building the networks that are so important to legislative success. More time may better afford them the opportunity build the weak ties that are critical to effective legislating (Kirkland 2011) as opposed to legislators who have little time or staff to devote to such efforts. Conversely, Squire (1998) shows that legislative professionalism has a negative impact on the number of bills a legislature enacts per day. It could be that with more time and staff to devote to legislating, legislators and committees spend more time examining legislation that is put before them. One can imagine legislators in New Hampshire having little time (and no staff) to vigorously review proposals before them, leading to deference to committees or to fellow legislators, particularly those in positions of power or experience. Conversely, legislators with more resources, while still probably not likely to read all proposals before them, may have the luxury of greater scrutiny. As a result, legislative professionalism may affect the activity and success of legislators and committees.

Term Limits

Proponents of term limits proposed them with the expectation that they would alter how the legislature operates, in addition to changing who serves. And indeed, term limits have been found to have numerous effects on the legislators, committees, and the legislative process, although these effects are not necessarily what supporters would have predicted (Carey et al. 2006; Kousser 2005; Sarbaugh-Thompson et al. 2004). Term limits have been shown to shift power away from the legislature towards other actors such as the governor and bureaucracy (Carey et al. 2006) and lead to term limited legislators expending less effort on legislating, as measured by roll call participation (Wright 2007). However, legislators' self-reports suggest they spend less time on electoral activities, leaving more time for legislating (Carey et al. 2006). Cain and Kousser (2004, vi) find that term limits in Washington led committees to screen out fewer bills assigned to them; they were also shown less deference when their reports hit the floor, both in terms of lower passage rates and increased amendment activity.

Thus, there are several ways term limits may alter the costs and benefits associated with legislating. First, because the electoral connection is attenuated in a term limited legislature, the opportunity and electoral costs of legislating may be lower for those serving in these institutions (Carey et al. 2006). Legislators may see less potential electoral risk in proposing controversial matters or signing on to legislation of their peers. There may be potential personal benefits as well, particularly if other actors, such as interest groups or lobbyists, ask for such favors. As such, legislators may be more active overall.

Conversely, to the extent that legislating becomes less costly as one gains experience with the process, term limits may raise the actual costs of legislating, as effect confirmed in other countries (Dal Bo and Rossi 2008). With each electoral cycle, experienced legislators depart, and inexperienced legislators assume the responsibility of figuring out how the legislative process works. Furthermore, to the extent that co-sponsorship is an indication of the connectedness of legislators (Kirkland 2011), there may be reduced co-sponsorship levels overall in term limited states. Because legislators in these states will have less time to build these networks, particularly the weak ties, which Kirkland (2011) shows are particularly important in legislatures, then it seems likely that there will be less co-sponsorship. Similarly, the presence of term limits may be negatively related to legislative effectiveness, as less extensive networks mean less built-in support for sponsored legislation. So term limits could lead to reduced activity overall.

Term limits may also condition the effect of seniority in these legislatures. In non-term limited states, legislators with four years of experience may not be all that different from legislators with six years of experience, but in a term limited state like Ohio, the latter legislator will at the peak of his or her legislative experience; thus, the impact of seniority should be more pronounced in term limited states as these limits serve to amplify these benefits associated with seniority.

Limits on Legislative Process: Signature Limits, Co-Sponsor Deadlines, Limited Introductions, and Introduction Deadlines

Across the states, a variety of legislatures have rules that limit the legislative process; some of these limits are established in statute, while some are enshrined in the state constitution. As the NSCL (1996) notes, the goal of these limits is explicitly to alter the legislative process, typically by slowing it down or by reducing the number of bills introduced. These limits are really barriers that raise the cost of legislating for members of the institution.

For instance, deadlines for bill introductions reduce the time available for legislating—and there are only 24 hours in a day, and some things may not be put off until later. The NSCL (1996) identifies a number of limits on the legislative process including limits on the number of cosponsors that a sponsor may obtain, deadlines for cosponsor signatures, limits on the number of bills that may be introduced by any legislator, and deadlines on introductions.

Generally speaking, limits on the legislative process should have negative relationships with both activity and effectiveness as they raise the cost of legislating. Indeed, Squire (1998) shows that introduction limits have a negative impact on the overall productivity of legislatures. But different rules should be related to different types of activity in potentially different ways. Obviously, limits on introductions should be negatively related to the number of bills that are lead sponsored, simply because legislators in these states cannot sponsor any more bills than the rule allows. Likewise, limits on co-sponsorship, such as co-sponsor deadlines and signature limits, should have a negative impact on co-sponsorship activity. However, they may have a positive impact on effectiveness, as legislators may be less likely to sign on to any bill and sponsors may seek to sign only those most likely to positively impact the passage of the bill.

Leader Tools

As noted above, past research has demonstrated that party leaders tend to be more active sponsors of bills, but less active as co-sponsors. However, little research has examined how the tools available to these leaders condition this finding. In addition, these tools may also shape the actions of others, as research has demonstrated that leaders can use these powers to shape the actions of other actors (Grumm 1964; Jenkins 2008; Scully and Patterson 1997; Volden and Bergman 2006). Leaders use tools like control of the calendar to shape the actions of individuals in the chamber, in particular to reduce the rate at which the party is rolled (Anzia and Jackman 2013) and the rate at which individual members vote together (Jenkins 2008). Indeed, control of these tools is seen as fundamental to party control of the legislative process (Aldrich 1995; Aldrich and Rohde 1997; Cooper and Brady 1981; Cox and McCubbins 1993; Kiewiet and McCubbins 1991; Smith 2000). Of course, there is a difference between the tools that are provided to party leaders and their effectiveness in using them (Battista 2011; Mooney 2010), but these tools still matter. Measures of these tools typically include a leader's power to appoint committee chairs and members, to refer and schedule bills, and to control resources like staff and extra compensation (Mooney 2010, 8).

The first effect of these leader tools should be on the activity and effectiveness of party leaders. There are two distinct hypotheses that emerge with respect to these tools. On the one hand, these tools may straight-forwardly enhance the activity and effectiveness of party leaders as they use these powers to enhance their own legislative prospects. On the other hand, having more of these tools may lead to lower levels of activity and effectiveness for individual party leaders. This may seem counter-intuitive at first, but leaders who have more tools will be able to rely on those tools to shape the legislative process to their liking. Conversely, leaders with few tools may have to resort to actually proposing legislation (and securing passage of said legislation) in order to shape outcomes. This points to a potential secondary effect of party leader tools through majority party status. As noted above, central to many theories of party control of government is the idea that party members empower leaders to enhance the prospects of majority party members. Thus, it seems reasonable to presume that increased leader tools will positively affect the activity and success of majority party members and negatively affect minority party members. Leaders use the tools given to them to get members to toe the party line—this is why they empower leaders. The assumption is that these powers will help the party overcome collective action problems, leading to more success both for the party and for individual party members.

Committee Powers

In addition to influencing the actions of individual legislators, the political conditions and institutional arrangements should also alter the behavior of committees; specifically, those rules that empower committees should lead to a greater role for committees in the legislative process. Research has shown that the powers of these committees, including the ability to decline to hear bills or to decline to report them to the floor, matters for things like the rate at which parties are rolled (Anzia and Jackman 2013). However, comparative analyses of committee power in state legislatures shows variation in the independence and rights of committees in state legislatures (Hamm, Hedlund and Martorano 2006; Martorano 2006), which has made it difficult to fully assess their role in the legislative process.

Nonetheless, it is important to look at how these rules influence the role committees play in receiving and passing out legislation as these rules clearly constrain committee activity. The key rules constraining or empowering committees in state legislatures include: whether committees must hear all bills, who determines which bills are heard in committees with discretion (usually the chair, but committee members or bill authors play some role in some states), who determines when bills are heard (in some states, committees must hear bills chronologically), whether a committee has explicit power to kill bills (some may only postpone indefinitely for instance), and whether a committee must report on bills referred to them (ASLCS and NCSL 1991). Committees with more powers should report out fewer bills, as rules empowering their discretion should lead them to act in this way. Furthermore, the floor should be more deferential to committees with these powers. As with party leaders, this is presumably why the floor empowers committees—to achieve collective goals. When these powers are given to committees, legislators should then be more inclined to support the decisions these committees make.

Some rules constrain committee discretion; they may make committees more active though. For example, some chambers require that all bills must be heard; this will surely increase the number of bills being heard by committees, as leaders will have less ability to allow bills to die before reaching committees. Committees required to report on all bills will also surely have higher report rates due to this rule, although Squire and Moncrief (2010) note there are "quirks and oddities" in the legislative process in almost every state as legislatures sometimes seek to bypass these limits. For example, after the passage of the GAVEL amendment, which required a committee vote on all bills referred to them, the locus of killing power did not disappear; instead, it shifted to the Appropriations Committee in the Colorado House (Binder, Kogan, and Kousser 2011). Thus, report rates should increase when committees have less discretion and power. Ultimately, then, rules that empower committees should lead them to play a larger role in the legislative process, hearing more bills and reporting fewer bills as compared to other chambers where they and leaders have less discretion, as these rules should reduce the costs of committee activity.

Conclusion

Legislators and other actors within institutions are calculating, and they carefully consider the implications of their actions. With limited time and resources, decisions must be made in order to determine how to most effectively allocate them. These decisions will shape the time, effort, and resources put into legislating, as opposed to other potential activities. However, it is plain to see that these decisions are not made in a vacuum. The context of legislating matters as environmental features will raise or lower the costs of different types of legislative work for different types of actors. For example, the GAVEL amendment significantly reduced the ability of the majority party and committee chairs to control the legislative process, raising the cost of legislative activity for these actors. Conditions changed, and legislators, leaders, and committees responded (Binder, Kogan, and Kousser 2011). The effects of these rules, resources, and political conditions are complicated and varied; for instance, rules that raise the cost of one type of activity for one set of legislators may lower the cost of another type of activity for different legislators. Term limits may lower the costs of legislating for junior legislators, leading to more primary sponsorship, but they may also reduce the effectiveness of more senior legislators in these institutions. Understanding these effects is critical to developing a clear picture of the legislative process, an effort started in the next chapter which beings at the beginning: initiating legislation.

Notes

1 Information about the GAVEL ballot initiative and results comes from the National Conference of State Legislatures Ballot Measures Database.

2 While the research identifies these as institutional features, it is probably more accurate to say these are institutional positions for individual legislators as research typically does not look at how the power of associated with these positions varies. Rather, a dummy variable is commonly created to indicate if a legislator holds one of these positions or not. Additionally, scholars often place seniority in the category of institutional factors; this decision stems from the view that seniority confers upon legislators' institutional benefits. However, this assumes that all legislatures confer benefits on more senior members; this assumption stems from the fact that most studies of legislative effectiveness examine Congress, where this proposition holds true. But it may be the case that seniority carries few institutional benefits, say in a term-limited institution. Thus, it is more accurate to place seniority in the member characteristics category as it reflects what Miquel and Snyder (2006) term the acquisition of human capital through learning by doing.

3 There are a few studies that examine these questions in multiple legislative institutions. In particular, studies of legislative effectiveness are somewhat common. However, these studies tend to only examine a sample of bills in these institutions, such women's interest or black interest bills (Barnello and Bratton 2007; Bratton and Haynie 1999) or childhood obesity prevention (Boehmer et al. 2008).

4 Both of those changes were implemented after the period under examination here, so in reality, none of these chambers changed those rules from 1996 to the session under examination here.

5 Ideally, this analysis would include additional state level variables. However, since data was collected for ten states, this limits the number of state level variables that can be included in these models. A number of other state level variables were considered and tested. For example, chamber size could potentially impact success, as it may be more difficult to weed through the additional bills that come with more members, and it may be more difficult to build coalitions in institutions with more people, where individual ties may be weaker. Another variable considered was limits on the length of sessions; legislators may simply run out of time needed to process all bills, leading to fewer

introductions and less success. Given the limits on the number of state variables, some line had to be drawn, so careful consideration was given to a variety of state level variables, and only those with the strongest theoretical and practical relationship to these phenomena of interest were included. So for example, chamber size was dropped as other variables had stronger theoretical connections to these outcomes, and it was not significantly related to the dependent variables when included in these models. The same is true for session limits. Furthermore, the number of legislative days is one of three key components in Squire's (2007) measure of legislative professionalism, so this is already accounted for in these models. Finally, one of the limits on the legislative process, discussed below, includes deadlines for introductions, which is another way to measure whether legislators have limited time to introduce bills. Ultimately then, this concept is covered in other measures, so those measures were included instead.

6   This does not necessarily mean that threats to this system never occur. Indeed, in 2015, Senate President Stanley Rosenberg threatened to withdraw from the joint rules and committee system if the House did not agree to rules changes that reduced the House's advantage in this system (Rosenberg 2015). However, because the pull of tradition is strong, the House accepted these rules changes, rather than abandoning the joint system altogether.

7   Data in this paragraph is for the 2012 session and comes from the National Conference of State Legislatures.

References

Aldrich, John H. 1995. *Why Parties?* Chicago, IL: University of Chicago Press.

Aldrich, John and David Rohde. 1997. "Balance of Power: Republican Party Leadership and the Committee System in the 194th House." Presented at the annual meeting of the Midwest Political Science Association, Chicago, IL.

American Society of Legislative Clerks and Secretaries (ASLCS) and National Conference of State Legislatures (NCSL). 1991. *Inside the Legislative Process.* Denver, CO: National Conference of State Legislatures.

Anderson, William D., Janet Box-Steffensmeier, and Valeria Sinclair-Chapman. 2003. "The Keys to Legislative Success in the U.S. House of Representatives." *Legislative Studies Quarterly* 28: 357–386.

Anzia, Sarah F. and Molly C. Jackman. 2013. "Legislative Organization and the Second Face of Power: Evidence from U.S. State Legislatures." *Journal of Politics* 75: 210–224.

Barnello, Michelle and Kathleen A. Bratton. 2007. "Bridging the Gender Gap in Bill Sponsorship." *Legislative Studies Quarterly* 32 (3): 449–474.

Battista, James Coleman. 2004. "Reexamining Legislative Committee Repre-sentativeness in the States." *State Politics and Policy Quarterly* 4: 161–180.

——. 2006a. "Committee Theories and Committee Votes: Internal Committee Behavior in the California Legislature." *State Politics and Policy Quarterly* 6 (2): 151–173.

——. 2006b. "Jurisdiction, Institutional Structure, and Committee Representa-tiveness." *Political Research Quarterly* 59: 47–56.

———. 2009. "Why Information? Choosing Committee Informativeness in U.S. State Legislatures." *Legislative Studies Quarterly* 34: 375–397.

———. 2011. "Formal and Perceived Leadership Power in U.S. State Legislatures." *State Politics & Policy Quarterly* 11: 102–118.

Binder, Mike, Vladimir Kogan, and Thad Kousser. 2011. "How G.A.V.E.L. Changed Party Politics in Colorado's General Assembly." In *State of Change: Colorado Politics in the Twenty-First Century,* John Straayer, Robert Duffy and Courtenay Daum (Eds.). Boulder, CO: University Press of Colorado.

Binder, Sarah A. 2003. *Stalemate: Causes and Consequences of Legislative Gridlock.* Washington, DC: Brookings Institution Press.

Boehmer, Tegan K., Douglas A. Luke, Debra L. Haire-Joshu, Hannalori S. Bates, and Ross C. Brownson. 2008. "Preventing Childhood Obesity Through State Policy: Predictors of Bill Enactment." *American Journal of Preventive Medicine* 34: 333–340.

Bowling, Cynthia J. and Margaret R. Ferguson. 2001. "Divided Government, Interest Representation, and Policy Differences: Competing Explanations of Gridlock in the Fifty States." *Journal of Politics* 63 (1): 182–206.

Brady, David W., Joseph Cooper, and Patricia A. Hurley. 1979. "The Decline of Party in the U.S. House of Representatives, 1887–1968." *Legislative Studies Quarterly* 4: 381–407.

Bratton, Kathleen A. and Kerry L. Haynie. 1999. "Agenda Setting and Legislative Success in State Legislatures: The Effects of Gender and Race." *Journal of Politics* 61 (3): 658–679.

Bratton, Kathleen A. and Stella M. Rouse. 2011. "Networks in the Legislative Arena: How Group Dynamics Affect Co-sponsorship." *Legislative Studies Quarterly* 36 (3): 423–460.

Browne, William P. 1985. "Multiple Sponsorship and Bill Success in State Legislatures." *Legislative Studies Quarterly* 10: 483–488.

Cain, Bruce E. and Thad Kousser. 2004. *Adapting to Term Limits: Recent Experiences and New Directions.* San Francisco, CA: Public Policy Institute of California.

Carey, John M., Richard G. Neimi, Lynda W. Powell, and Gary F. Moncrief. 2006. "The Effects of Term Limits on State Legislatures: A New Survey of the 50 States." *Legislative Studies Quarterly* 31 (1): 105–134.

Clucas, Richard C. 2003. "Improving the Harvest of State Legislative Research." *State Politics & Policy Quarterly* 3: 387–419.

Coleman, John J. 1999. "Unified Government, Divided Government, and Party Responsiveness." *American Political Science Review* 93: 821–835.

Coleman, John J. and David C. W. Parker. 1999. "The Consequences of Divided Government." In *The Oxford Handbook of the American Presidency,* George C. Edwards III and William G. Howell (Eds.). New York: Oxford University Press.

Cooper, Joseph, and David Brady. 1981. "Institutional Context and Leadership Style: The House from Cannon to Rayburn." *American Political Science Review* 75: 411–425.

Cox, Gary W. and Matthew D. McCubbins. 1993. *Legislative Leviathan: Party Government in the House.* Berkeley, CA: University of California Press.

Cox, Gary W. and William Terry. 2008. "Legislative Productivity in the 93rd–105th Congresses." *Legislative Studies Quarterly* 33: 1–16.

Crain, Mark W. and Robert D. Tollison. 1982. "Team Production in State Legislatures." *Micropolitics* 3: 111–121.

Dal Bo, Ernesto and Martin Rossi. 2008. "Term Length and Political Performance." Accessed at www.nber.org/papers/w14511 on June 13, 2014.

Deering, Christopher J. 1982. "Subcommittee Government in the U.S. House: An Analysis of Bill Management." *Legislative Studies Quarterly* 7: 533–546.

Ellickson, Mark C. 1992. "Pathways to Legislative Success: A Path Analytic Study of the Missouri House of Representatives." *Legislative Studies Quarterly* 17: 285–302.

Eulau, Heinz and Vera McCluggage. 1984. "Standing Committees in Legislatures: Three Decades of Research." *Legislative Studies Quarterly* 9 (2): 195–270.

Francis, Wayne L. 1989. *The Legislative Committee Game: A Comparative Analysis of 50 States.* Columbus, OH: Ohio State University Press.

Francis, Wayne L. and James W. Riddlesperger. 1982. "U.S. State Legislative Committees: Structure, Procedural Efficiency, and Party Control." *Legislative Studies Quarterly* 7: 453–471.

Frantzich, Stephen. 1979. "Who Makes Our Laws? The Legislative Effectiveness of Members of the U.S. Congress." *Legislative Studies Quarterly* 4: 409–428.

Garand, James C. and Kelly M. Burke. 2006. "Legislative Activity and the 1994 Republican Takeover: Exploring Changing Patterns of Sponsorship and Co-sponsorship in the U.S. House." *American Politics Research* 34: 159–188.

Gray, Virginia and David Lowery. 1995. "Interest Representation and Democratic Gridlock." *Legislative Studies Quarterly* 20 (4): 531–552.

Grumm, John G. 1964. "The Means of Measuring Conflict and Cohesion in the Legislature." *Southwestern Social Science Quarterly* 44: 377–388.

Hamm, Keith E., Robert Harmel and Robert Thompson. 1983. "Ethnic and Partisan Minorities in Two Southern State Legislatives." *Legislative Studies Quarterly* 8: 177–189.

Hamm, Keith E., Ronald D. Hedlund, and Nancy Martorano. 2006. "Measuring State Legislative Committee Power: Change and Chamber Differences in the 20th Century." *State Politics and Policy Quarterly* 6: 88–111.

Hasecke, Edward B. and Jason D. Mycoff. 2007. "Party Loyalty and Legislative Success: Are Loyal Majority Party Members More Successful in the U.S. House of Representatives." *Political Research Quarterly* 60: 607–617.

Hedlund, Ronald D. and Keith E. Hamm. 1996. "Political Parties as Vehicles for Organizing U.S. State Legislative Committees." *Legislative Studies Quarterly* 21: 383–408.

Hicks, William D. and Daniel A. Smith. 2009. "Do Parties Matter? Explaining Legislative Productivity in American States." Paper presented at the State of the Parties: 2008 & Beyond Conference, Akron, OH.

Jackman, Molly. 2014. "Parties, Median Legislators, and Agenda Setting: How Legislative Institutions Matter." *Journal of Politics* 76: 259–272.

Jenkins, Shannon. 2008. "Party Influence on Roll Call Voting: A View from the U.S. States." *State Politics and Policy Quarterly* 8 (3): 239–262.

Jeydel, Alana and Andrew J. Taylor. 2003. "Are Women Legislators Less Effective? Evidence from the U.S. House in the 103th–105th Congress." *Political Research Quarterly* 56: 19–27.

Jewell, Malcolm E. 1962. *The State Legislature: Politics and Practice.* New York: Random House.

——. 1986. "Dimensions of Partisanship in State Legislatures." Presented at the Hendricks Symposium on Legislative Organizations, University of Nebraska, Lincoln, NE.

Kiewiet, D. Roderick and Mathew D. McCubbins. 1991. *The Logic of Delegation: Congressional Parties and the Appropriations Process.* Chicago, IL: University of Chicago Press.

Kirkland, Justin H. 2011. "The Relational Determinants of Legislative Outcomes: Strong and Weak Ties Between Legislators." *Journal of Politics* 73 (3): 887–898.

Koger, Gregory. 2003. "Position Taking and Co-sponsorship in the House." *Legislative Studies Quarterly* 28 (2): 225–246.

Kousser, Thad. 1995. "Co-sponsors and Wafflers from A to Z." *American Journal of Political Science* 39: 906–923.

——. 1996. "Institutional and Partisan Sources of Gridlock: A Theory of Divided and Unified Government." *Journal of Theoretical Politics* 8: 7–40.

——. 2005. *Term Limits and the Dismantling of Legislative Professionalism.* New York: Cambridge University Press.

——. 2010. "Does Party Polarization Lead to Policy Gridlock in California?" *California Journal of Politics and Policy* 2 (2): 1–23.

Krutz, Glen S. 2005. "Issues and Institutions: 'Winnowing' in the U.S. Congress." *American Journal of Political Science* 49: 313–326.

Maestas, Cherie. 2000. "Professional Legislatures and Ambitious Politicians: Policy Responsiveness of Individuals and Institutions." *Legislative Studies Quarterly* 25: 663–690.

Maltzman, Forrest. 1997. *Competing Principals: Committees, Parties and the Organization of Congress.* Ann Arbor, MI: University of Michigan Press.

Martorano, Nancy. 2006. "Balancing Power: Committee System Autonomy and Legislative Organization." *Legislative Studies Quarterly* 31: 205–234.

Mayhew, David. 2002. *Divided We Govern: Party Control, Lawmaking, and Investigations.* New Haven, CT: Yale University Press.

Miquel, Gerard Padro I. and James M. Snyder. 2006. "Legislative Effectiveness and Legislative Careers." *Legislative Studies Quarterly* 31: 347–381.

Mooney, Christopher Z. 2010. "Principals, Agents, Tools and Influence: The Dynamic of Disappointment in Legislative Leadership Influence." Paper Presented at the 2010 American Political Science Association Annual Meeting, Washington, DC.

National Conference of State Legislatures (NCSL). 1996. Accessed at www.ncsl.org/documents/legismgt/ILP/96Tab3Pt1.pdf on October 23, 2015.

Osborn, Tracy. 2003. "Patterns in Roll Call Voting among Women State Legislators." Paper Presented at the 2003 American Political Science Association Annual Meeting, Chicago, IL.

Overby, Marvin L. and Thomas A. Kazee. 2000. "Outlying Committees in the Statehouse: An Examination of the Prevalence of Committee Outliers in State Legislatures." *Journal of Politics* 62: 701–728.

Overby, Marvin L. , Thomas A. Kazee, and David W. Prince. 2004. "Committee Outliers in State Legislatures." *Legislative Studies Quarterly* 29: 81–107.

Platt, Matthew. 2008. "Legislative Problem-Solving: Exploring Bill Sponsorship in Post-War America." Accessed at www.people.fas.harvard.edu/~mplatt/ Documents/Bill%20Introduction%20Paper.pdf on June 4, 2014.

Prince, David W. and L. Marvin Overby. 2005. "Legislative Organization Theory and Committee Preference Outliers in State Senates." *State Politics and Policy Quarterly* 5: 68–87.

Reingold, Beth. 2000. *Representing Women: Sex, Gender, and Legislative Behavior in Arizona and California.* Chapel Hill, NC: University of North Carolina Press.

Richman, Jesse. 2008. "Uncertainty and the Prevalence of Committee Outliers." *Legislative Studies Quarterly* 33: 323–347.

Rocca, Michael S. and Gabriel R. Sanchez. 2008. "The Effect of Race and Ethnicity on Bill Sponsorship and Co-sponsorship in Congress." *American Politics Research* 36 (1): 130–152.

Rogers, James R. 2002. "Free Riding in State Legislatures." *Public Choice* 113 (1–2): 59–76.

Rosenberg, Stanley. 2015. "Message on Joint Rules." Accessed at www.stan rosenberg.com/article/message-joint-rules on October 9, 2015.

Rosenthal, Alan. 1973. "Legislative Committee Systems: An Exploratory Analysis." *Western Political Quarterly* 26: 252–262.

———. 2008. *Engines of Democracy: Politics and Policymaking in State Legislatures.* Washington, DC: CQ Press.

Ryan, Josh M. 2014. "Conference Committee Proposal Rights and Policy Outcomes in the States." *Journal of Politics* 76: 1059–1073.

Saint-Germain, Michelle. 1989. "Does Their Difference Make a Difference?: The Impact of Women on Public Policy in the Arizona State Legislature." *Social Science Quarterly* 70: 956–969.

Sarbaugh-Thompson, Marjorie, Lyke Thompson, Charles D. Elder, John Strate, and Richard Elling. 2004. *The Political and Institutional Effects of Term Limits.* New York: Palgrave Macmillan.

Schiller, Wendy J. 1995. "Senators as Political Entrepreneurs: Using Bill Sponsorship to Shape Legislative Agendas." *American Journal of Political Science* 39 (1): 186–203.

Scully, Roger M. and Samuel C. Patterson. 1997. "Ideological Thinking in Legislative Decision Making." Paper Presented at the Annual Meeting of the Midwest Political Science Association, Chicago, IL, April 10–12, 1997.

Sinclair, Barbara Deckard. 1977. "Determinants of Aggregate Party Cohesion in the U.S. House of Representatives, 1901–1956." *Legislative Studies Quarterly* 2: 155–175.

Smith, Steven S. 2000. "Positive Theories of Congressional Parties." *Legislative Studies Quarterly* 25: 193–215.

Squire, Peverill and Keith E. Hamm. 2005. *101 Chambers: Congress, State Legislatures, and the Future of Legislative Studies*. Columbus, OH: Ohio State University Press.

Squire, Peverill and Gary Moncrief. 2010. *State Legislatures Today: Politics Under the Domes*. Boston, MA: Longman.

Squire, Peverill. 1998. "Membership Turnover and the Efficient Processing of Legislation." *Legislative Studies Quarterly* 32 (1): 23–32.

———. 2007. "Measuring Legislative Professionalism: The Squire Index Revisited." *State Politics and Policy Quarterly* 7: 211–227.

Stewart, Charles III. 2001. *Analyzing Congress, 2nd edition*. New York: W.W. Norton & Company.

———. 2002. *The Difference Women Make: The Policy Impact of Women in Congress*. Chicago, IL: University of Chicago Press.

Thomas, Sue. 1991. "The Impact of Women on State Legislative Politics." *Journal of Politics* 53: 958–976.

———. 1994. *How Women Legislate*. New York: Oxford University Press.

Van Der Slik, Jack R. and Kent Redfield. 1986. *Lawmaking in Illinois: Legislative Politics, People, and Processes*. Springfield, IL: Sangamon State University.

Volden, Craig and Elizabeth Bergman. 2006. "How Strong Should Our Party Be? Party Member Preferences over Party Cohesion." *Legislative Studies Quarterly* 31: 71–104.

Volden, Craig and Alan E. Wiseman. 2007. "Legislative Effectiveness in Congress." Paper Presented at the 2007 Annual Meeting of the American Political Science Association, Chicago, IL.

Volden, Craig, Alan E. Wiseman, and Dana E. Wittmer. 2013. "Are Women More Effective Lawmakers Than Men?" *American Journal of Political Science* 57: 326–341.

Wilson, Rick K. and Cheryl D. Young. 1997. "Co-sponsorship in the U.S. Congress." *Legislative Studies Quarterly* 22: 25–43.

Wright, Gerald C. 2007. "Do Term Limits Affect Legislative Roll Call Voting." *State Politics and Policy Quarterly* 7 (3): 256–280.

3 Initiating Legislation

Two legislators with similar backgrounds (white, male, Republican rank-and-file members serving in a Democratic institution, elected just one election cycle apart) served as representatives in the 2007–2008 legislative session. Each legislator served as lead sponsor on six bills, but one of the legislators signed on to co-sponsor just eight of his colleagues' bills, while the other legislator signed on to co-sponsor 534 of his colleagues' proposals. Two black, male, Democratic party leaders and committee chairs in two other chambers had vastly different patterns of activity; in one chamber, one of these legislators lead sponsored six bills and co-sponsored five, while in another chamber, the other legislator served as lead sponsor to 37 bills and signed on as a co-sponsor to 87 more. During the same term, a party leader in one chamber sponsored just one amendment, while another party leader in a different chamber sponsored 59 amendments.

In legislatures across the country, legislators must make decisions about how to allocate their time and effort in the task of legislating. Sometimes, these legislators make similar choices, but often as the above examples illustrate, legislators make vastly different choices about how and when to sign on to legislative proposals and how much effort they will make to secure the passage of a particular proposal. The individual attributes of legislators play a role here, but as noted in the previous chapter, the characteristics of legislative institutions play a role as well, with factors such as the institutional resources available to legislators and rules that constrain the legislative process shaping the choices made by these individuals. Indeed, in the examples above, all of the personal attributes that research has shown to influence legislative activity are generally similar; what is different is the fact that each legislator in the pairs above served in different legislative institutions. The decisions these legislators make about legislating do not occur in a vacuum. Rather, they are shaped by contextual factors that serve to raise or lower the costs of legislative activity. Therefore, in understanding how legislative context shapes the legislative process, the first place to start is to examine how context shapes the activity of individual legislators engaged in initiating different types of legislation.

Initiating Legislation

Legislators engage in a variety of activities, of which legislating is only one. As Frantizch (1979, 409) notes in talking about Congress:

> Among other things, congressmen are expected to pass legislation, oversee the bureaucracy, mediate between constituents and the bureaucracy, serve as a sounding board for ideas, symbolize open and democratic government, and run for political office.

Of course, legislating is an important activity; indeed, legislators often indicate that legislating is the most important aspect of their job (Frantzich 1979, Rosenthal 2004). But as noted previously, the amount of time legislators have to devote to this activity is not unlimited, so legislators must determine how they are going to allocate the amount of time they have to the task of legislating and which issues they will address when legislating. In determining how much time to allocate to legislating and on which types of legislative activity to focus, the effect of factors that influence these decisions, both individual and contextual, may not be consistent across different types of legislative activity. Importantly, the costs associated with legislating vary across types of activity thus the need for resources may vary. Furthermore, the rules within institutions can target different types of activities, such as limits on the number of bills that legislators can introduce versus limits on the number of sponsors that can sign on the specific bills. The former should affect lead sponsorship, while the latter should affect co-sponsorship. So it is important to understand how these patterns of legislative activity vary across different institutions in order to begin to understand how they might be shaped by contextual factors.

To start, legislators are generally expected to put forward at least some of their own initiatives. But lead sponsorship is a costly activity (Schiller 1995). As Rosenthal (2004, 78) notes, "the workload is heavy and time is usually in short supply." Sponsors must bring resources to bear to craft and build support for a proposal; in doing so, there are opportunity costs involved as time spent on one activity cannot be spent engaging in others. As Rosenthal (2008, 330–331) notes, unless someone steps forward to move a bill through the process, the bill is likely to die; that someone is generally the lead sponsor of the bill. Furthermore, moving the bill through the process is not an easy task; there are numerous steps in all legislative chambers and the assent of the majority of a variety of actors must be obtained. Resources such as time in session and staff may help legislators bear the burden of these costs.

However, to the extent that legislators see legislating as the central focus of their job and believe it is necessary to engage in this activity to some degree, there should be more consistency in this activity across institutions: all legislatures and, to some degree, all legislators must legislate. Resources may help increase the volume of initiated legislation, but there is probably some minimal level of participation expected here. To the extent this is the most costly type of legislative activity (as opposed to co-sponsorship) though, there may be some upper limit here, where one simply runs out of time in the day. Therefore, there should be some variation across contexts in lead sponsorship, but not as much as compared to other types of less costly activities.

The data in Table 3.1 reveal this is, indeed, the case. There is far less variation in measures of lead sponsorship as compared to co-sponsorship. Across all states, the standard deviation for lead sponsorship is 9.76 as compared to 194.30 for co-sponsorship. The lowest average for lead sponsorship is 5.4 in Vermont, while the highest is 21.33 in Oregon, for a difference of only approximately 16 bills.[1]

Like lead sponsorship, amendment sponsorship is also a costly activity. To be sure, there are situations where legislators may propose amendments to make a point or to act as a poison pill in an attempt to defeat a bill, requiring little time and effort. But interviews with legislative clerks in these chambers suggest this is not common; indeed; close to three-quarters (72.8 percent) of all the proposed amendments in these chambers ultimately passed. Thus, most amendments seem to be proposed genuinely, and proposed amendments that are driven by a desire to improve upon or to secure a majority coalition for an existing proposal also induce resource costs, as sponsors of said amendments need to craft these proposals carefully and work to build support for them. As such, activity levels should be lower in this area, generally speaking, but once again, resources may help legislators bear the burden of these costs. Party leaders, who may be in a better position to broker compromise by offering legislators resources in order to induce compromise, should be more active in sponsoring amendments. Furthermore, to the extent that a chamber is deferent to committees (as informational theories of committees would suggest), committee chairs may become active stewards of bills that pass out of committee, and so these legislators may be more active in proposing amendments as well.

As Table 3.1 shows, legislators are indeed least active in this area, sponsoring an average of 3.4 amendments across all five institutions that report this data. As a result, there is less variation on the average number of amendments sponsored in these states, as the high ranges from just over 14

Table 3.1 Activity Levels in State Legislatures

State	Lead Sponsorship	Co-Sponsorship	Amendments Sponsored
Arkansas	16.11 Avg. 0 Min. 59 Max. 9.94 SD	45.25 Avg. 21 Min. 82 Max. 11.05 SD	7.22 Avg. 0 Min. 29 Max. 6.39 SD
Delaware	12.05 Avg. 1 Min. 44 Max. 11.14 SD	64.91 Avg. 6 Min. 127 Max. 21.75 SD	6.27 Avg. 0 Min. 27 Max. 6.59 SD
Georgia	8.09 Avg. 0 Min. 38 Max. 6.86 SD	25.29 Avg. 2 Min. 93 Max. 16.36 SD	UA
Indiana	8.18 Avg. 0 Min. 18 Max. 4.64 SD	9.06 Avg. 0 Min. 40 Max. 6.43 SD	2.1 Avg. 0 Min. 13.00 Max. 2.57 SD
Ohio	7.04 Avg. 0 Min. 21 Max. 5.15 SD	61.41 Avg. 0 Min. 207 Max. 43.04 SD	UA
Oregon	21.33 Avg. 4 Min. 64 Max. 14.68 SD	71.92 Avg. 21 Min. 136 Max. 27.84 SD	UA
Pennsylvania	13.62 Avg. 0 Min. 78 Max. 10.89 SD	416.69 Avg. 19 Min. 1879 Max. 288.29 SD	UA
Vermont	5.40 Avg. 0 Min. 25 Max. 5.29 SD	31.87 Avg. 1 Min. 65 Max. 13.20 SD	.80 Avg. 0 Min. 7 Max. 1.33 SD
Wisconsin	9.32 Avg. 0 Min. 55 Max. 8.61 SD	105.40 Avg. 15 Min. 386 Max. 79.42 SD	4.17 Avg. 0 Min. 35 Max. 5.13 SD
Wyoming	6.30 Avg. 0 Min. 18 Max. 4.51 SD	18.29 Avg. 4 Min. 47 Max. 9.53 SD	14.10 Avg. 0 Min. 61 Max. 13.05 SD
Total	10.59 Avg. 0 Min. 78 Max. 9.76 SD	113.14 Avg. 1897 Min. 47 Max. 194.30 SD	4.66 Avg. 0 Min. 61 Max. 7.15 SD

Note: UA = Data unavailable on the state legislative website

in Wyoming to a low of just under one in Vermont. The standard deviation of 7.15 and the average of 4.66 on this measure are the lowest for all of the measures of activity. Furthermore, it is far more common for legislators to display no activity in this area, as compared to lead sponsorship and co-sponsorship. Of this sample for which amendment data is available (for 554 legislators), 30.3 percent of them (or 168) sponsored no amendments at all.

However, legislative norms about who should bear responsibility for this task appear to vary across institutions, demonstrating the need to consider context in understanding the legislative process. For example, in Arkansas, 90.4 percent of amendments to bills were introduced by the lead sponsor of that bill, and of the 83 amendments that were not offered by the lead sponsor, 49 of them were offered by the Joint Budget Committee. So, just under four percent of these amendments were offered by legislators who were not lead sponsors of the bill.

But while the task of amending bills falls primarily to the primary sponsors of bills in some chambers, it falls to those actors who have more resources and power in the institution, namely party leaders and committee chairs, in other chambers. For instance, in Wyoming, close to 62 percent of the 361 amendments proposed were introduced by a committee chair or party leader. The chair of the Joint Appropriations committee Wyoming managed to secure the passage of 53 of the 61 amendments he sponsored. Budget bills, of all bills considered in legislative chambers, are probably the most commonly amended bills. This is true in Arkansas, where committees themselves may offer amendments to bills; the most active amendment sponsor in the chamber is the Joint Budget Committee, which offered 111 (12.8 percent) of the 868 amendments proposed during this session.

Thus, even a brief descriptive analysis of amendment sponsorship and passage in these chambers shows there are different patterns for this type of activity and these patterns vary across chambers. And as Chapter 5 reveals, these differing norms influence whether legislators are successful in securing passage of these amendments too. Nonetheless, one commonality that emerges here is that it is not typical for legislators who do not have a strong commitment to a bill or who do not have power in a chamber to sponsor amendments.

Co-sponsorship, on the other hand, is generally a less costly activity as compared to these other types of legislative activity. Co-sponsorship is seen as an important position-taking activity that serves as a signaling device to attentive actors such as other legislators, interest groups, or even constituents (Highton and Rocca 2005; Kessler and Krehbiel 1996; Kirkland 2011; Krutz 2005). Kessler and Krehbiel (1996, 555) deem this position taking activity "low-cost" because legislators do not have to engage in the hard work of moving a bill forward through the process.

Of course, while co-sponsorship is generally lower cost than lead sponsorship across these chambers, the extent to which co-sponsorship is truly a low cost activity and a signaling device across institutions is an open question. Ultimately, the meaning and the costs associated with this activity may vary across institution. For example, in studying the U.S. House, Garand and Burke (2006, 162) note that the costs of sponsorship and co-sponsorship will vary across legislators, but it may also be the case that the costs of these activities will vary across institutions, too. Garand and Burke (2006, 165) continue to note legislators must "tailor their activities based on the environments in which they reside." In some institutions, co-sponsorship may entail nothing more than signing your name to a bill. What matters is the number of signatures you have on a bill, more than who those signatories are. For instance, in the U.S. House, members have been known to withdraw co-sponsorship or even vote against their own proposals when the political winds change (Krehbiel 1995; Garand and Burke 2006).

Pennsylvania appears to be a prime example of an institution where co-sponsorship is a low-cost activity for those signing on to bills, as legislators in this institution are far more active in this arena as compared to other legislators as shown in Table 3.1. For example, in Pennsylvania, the maximum number of bills co-sponsored for an individual legislator was 1,879; six legislators in this chamber co-sponsored over 1,000 bills each, and 65 legislators sponsored over 500 bills. If the legislator who co-sponsored 1,879 bills worked on signing these propositions every day of the year, he would have signed an average of over five bills per day. But clearly, this legislator is not signing bills every day (including weekends!), so it does not seem possible that said legislator is actually reading all of these bills or potentially even thinking about co-sponsorship carefully. In this institution then, it does not appear that co-sponsors are asked to bear a large portion of the burden and so sign on more freely.

In other institutions, though, it may be the lead sponsors chose their co-sponsors carefully, looking for other members who have prestige or resources or who may be willing to share the burden of securing passage. This may be particularly true in those institutions that impose limits on the number of legislators that may co-sponsor proposals. In such an environment, the signaling importance of co-sponsorship may increase, such that lead sponsors may want to more carefully consider who makes the cut. For instance, the Indiana legislature limits the number of co-sponsors that may sign on to any one bill. This restriction appears to influence co-sponsorship activity in this chamber, as the average number of co-sponsored bills was slightly less than 10 bills per legislator. Over one-fifth of all legislators in this chamber co-sponsored four or fewer bills; in Pennsylvania, only one legislator co-sponsored fewer than 40 bills.

The descriptive statistics in Table 3.1 lend further support to the notion that the meaning and the costs associated with this activity may vary across institutions; the standard deviation for co-sponsorship levels across all states was over 194. Part of this is a reflection of the unusually high levels of co-sponsorship in Pennsylvania. The average numbers of bills sponsored in this chamber is 416, which is higher than the maximum number of co-sponsorships in all of the other states. But the standard deviation for this measure across the states excluding Pennsylvania is still 44.3, well above this measure for lead and amendment sponsorship activity.

Additionally, there is greater variability in the patterns in this measure across the states. For instance, the maximum number of bills co-sponsored by any one legislator in Indiana was 40; in Wyoming, it was 47. But in Pennsylvania, the maximum number of bills co-sponsored was 1,879, as noted above. This variability is still apparent even if Pennsylvania is excluded. The average number of co-sponsorships in Wisconsin is over 100—well above the average in Indiana, which is approximately nine bills per legislator.

Furthermore, a brief analysis of the bivariate relationships between measures of activity and the individual characteristics of legislators in these states shows there is variation across the states in the strength and direction of the relationship for all types of legislative activity as shown in Table 3.2. For example, majority party status is typically positively related to activity (as in Georgia for co-sponsorships), but it is also sometimes negatively related to activity (as in Ohio for the same measure). This is interesting, as research has shown that majority party status is one of the dominant explanations of legislative activity (Frantzich 1979; Garand and Burke 2006, Platt 2008). But these results show that these findings do not necessarily hold across all legislative institutions in the U.S. or across all types of legislative activity, particularly when analyses do not account for the sorts of contextual effects that may condition these relationships.

It is also important to look at different types of legislative activity as the characteristics of individual legislators are sometimes related to different measures of activity in different ways. For example, in Indiana, members of the majority party are significantly more likely to lead sponsor bills, but they are less likely to sponsor amendments, as Table 3.2 shows. In Delaware though, majority party members are significantly more likely to act as lead sponsors and to sponsor amendments. Seniority is positively related to lead sponsorship in Arkansas, but negatively related to co-sponsorship in the same chamber. But it is positively related to both sponsorship and co-sponsorship in Wisconsin. Even the committee chair variable, which is one of the more consistent variables here, is not related to all measures of activity in the same way across the states; committee chairs in Indiana are more likely to lead and co-sponsor bills, but less likely to sponsor amendments.

Table 3.2: Selected Correlations between Legislative Activity and Legislator Characteristics

	Majority Party			Seniority			Party Leader			Committee Chair		
	L	C	A	L	C	A	L	C	A	L	C	A
All States	.136***	–.024	.157**	–.009	–.090**	–.001	–.070*	.072*	–.093*	.354***	.304***	.236***
Arkansas	–.092	–.018	–.005	.424***	–.227*	.371***	.191^	.094	.169^	.379**	.011	.344***
Delaware	.318*	.155	.458**	.385**	.021	.258^	.182	–.103	.055	.515***	.464***	.568***
Georgia	.435***	.412***		–.017	–.041		–.044	.111		.366***	.317***	
Indiana	.437***	.122	–.306**	.002	–.048	–.062	–.256*	–.145	.008	.449***	.172^	–.208*
Ohio	.209*	–.271**		.144	–.039		–.518^	.161		.281**	–.207*	
Oregon	.028	.161		.077	–.183		.141	.041		.099	.001	
Pennsylvania	.131^	.084		–.037	–.125^		.150*	–.153*		.016	.154*	
Vermont	.116	.059	–.137^	.228**	–.116	.107	–.042	–.301***	.139^	.210**	–.039	.133
Wisconsin	.182^	.192^	.253*	.254*	.217*	.133	.005	–.132	–.058	.345***	.361***	.434***
Wyoming	.237^	–.143	.314*	.246^	–.031	.424**	.221^	.294*	.313*	.278*	–.103	.665***

Note: L = Lead sponsorship. C = Co-sponsorship. A = Amendment Sponsorship ^ p < .10, * p < .05, ** p < .01, *** p < .001

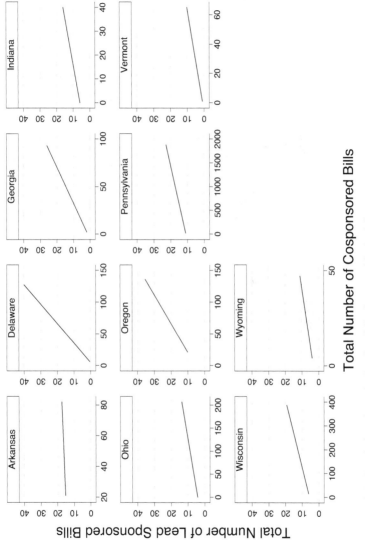

Figure 3.1 Correlations between Lead and Co-Sponsorship Activity

In addition, correlations between different measures of sponsorship in the states show that legislators who score highly on one measure do not always score highly on other measures, suggesting that different factors influence activity in these areas. As Figure 3.1 demonstrates, the strength of these correlations varies across the states. For instance, the relationship between lead and co-sponsorship is positive in all the states, but the slope of this relationship varies considerably. In states like Delaware and Oregon, there appears to be a strong relationship positive relationship between these types of activities; legislators who lead sponsor more bills also co-sponsor more bills. But in Arkansas, there appears to be little relationship between these two types of activities. Thus, it is important to examine both individual and institutional explanations for patterns of legislative activity and to look at these different types of behavior separately, as context may have different effects on different types of legislative activity.

Indeed, the likelihood ratio tests for all types of legislative activity, as shown in Table 3.3, indicate that there are significant state effects in the models; this is unsurprising given the variations in patterns of activity described above. [2] However, these tests also indicate the amount of variance explained by state level factors differs for the different types of activity. For instance, just over 30 percent of the variance in lead sponsorship activity is explained by state level variables, but close to 47 percent of the variance in the number of co-sponsored bills is explained by state level variables.

Clearly then, in looking simply at the patterns of activity across these chambers and across these states, two things are clear. First, levels of activity vary across types of legislative vehicles, and second, these patterns also vary across chambers. Contextual variables can help disentangle these relationship and lead to a better understanding about the causes of these patterns.

Table 3.3 Variance Tests for Significant State Effects in Legislative Activity

	Overall mean	*Variance Partition Coefficient (% variance at state level)*	*LR*
Lead Sponsorship	11.47	30.13	239.79**
Co-Sponsorship	85.23	46.9	880.2***
Amendment Sponsorship	5.767	38.40	186.07***

Note: ^ p < .10, * p < .05, ** p < .01, *** p < .001

Contextual Effects on Initiating Legislation

Due to the multi-level nature of the data (legislators nested in lower chambers), multi-level modeling will be used. Each model includes a set of individual level variables that research has shown to be related to legislative activity as outlined in Chapter 2. These variables are: party leadership, committee chair, seniority, majority party status, sex, and race (measured as whether the legislator was African American). With the exception of seniority, all of these measures are dummy variables; seniority is measured as the number of years since a given legislator was first elected or appointed. This data was collected mainly from the state legislative website, the chamber clerk, or the state's official elections website. Data on race was collected from the National Black Caucus of State Legislators; gender data come from the Center for American Women and Politics.

Next, each model will contain a set of institutional variables, corresponding to the categories of contextual factors outlined in Chapter 2, along with variables that capture the interaction between individual and state level variables. The political variables included in these models are party control, divided government and majority size. The first is a dummy variable indicating whether Democrats control the chamber; the second is a dummy variable that indicates whether one party controlled all three branches of government. Given that Democrats take a more expansive view of the role of government, the former variable should be positively related to initiation, while past research suggests that if divided government affects the quantity of legislation, it should do so in a negative way (Binder 2003; Coleman 1999; Gray and Lowery 1995; Kousser 2010). Finally, majority size is measured as the percent of seats held by the majority party in the chamber. Past research suggest that the average production of legislation in a state legislature decreases as majority size increases due to free riding (Rogers 2002), so this variable should be negative related to lead sponsorship. It may also be negatively related to co-sponsorship, although having more co-partisans may lead to increased opportunities to sign on, leading to a positive relationship.

Additionally, these multi-level models include a number of institutional variables related to the rules and resources in these chambers. Consistent with the factors identified in Chapter 2, variables included in this model are legislative professionalism (Squire 2007), term limits, legislative process limits (NCSL 1996), and leader tools (Mooney 2010). Past research suggests the effect of legislative professionalism may be positive, due to increased time to legislate (Clucas 2003) and increased time to build networks, but it may also be negative (Squire 1998) due to greater scrutiny that is possible with more time and resources.

The process limits were first identified from the National Conference of State Legislatures and the American Society of Legislative Clerks survey from 1996, then confirmed as still in effect with the House Clerk. These limits include: limits on the number of co-sponsors, deadlines for adding co-sponsors, limits on the number of bill introductions, and deadlines for bill introductions. There are other limits identified in the NCSL/ASCL report, but these mainly focus on when bills must pass through certain parts of the legislative process. As the focus here is on sponsorship and co-sponsorship, these other limits are not included. State values on this variable range from zero (Arkansas, Delaware, Ohio, and Wisconsin) to three (Indiana and Wyoming), as shown in Table 1.3. As these rules are intended to dampen the number of proposals in the pipeline, the expected effect of these rules is negative.

Of course, it is also expected that these contextual variables will have interactive effects; if these variables raise (or lower) the cost of legislating, then they will not do so equally for all legislators. For instance, term limits my serve to amplify the effects of seniority, and party related variables may alter the behavior of majority party members in particular. The effect of leader tools should operate primarily through cross-level interactions, as majority party members empower party leaders to help them accomplish party business (Anzia and Jackman 2013).

The multi-level models in Table 3.4 confirm that individual and institutional variables are important in explaining legislative activity and that institutional resources, rules and political conditions all condition the effect of individual level variables.[3] No variable is significant in every model, and there are some interesting effects, particularly for the cross-level interaction variables. Starting with the individual level variables, committee chairs and party leaders are, generally speaking, more active, as past research has shown and as Table 3.4 demonstrates. Even when controlling for institutional features, those with more resources tend to be more active generally. For instance, committee chairs sponsor almost four more bills, co-sponsor over 21 more bills and sponsor over four more amendments than non-chairs. Party leaders are more active as lead sponsors and putting forward amendments. However, they are considerably less active than their peers with respect to co-sponsorship, confirming past research. This is not altogether surprising; given limited amounts of time and the additional time demands of serving as a leader that time has to come from somewhere. It appears to come from co-sponsorship activity. The differing effects of being a party leader and being a committee chair are interesting though. Perhaps leaders are more focused on running the institution, while chairs are more focused on processing legislating, leading to the latter becoming more active with respect to co-sponsorship. But the time demands of leadership appear to mean there is less time to devote to co-sponsoring.

Table 3.4 Modeling Legislative Activity in the U.S. States

	Lead Sponsorship	Co–Sponsorship	Amendment Sponsorship
Individual Level Variables			
Party Leader	11.397**	−103.712^	12.318***
	(3.691)	(56.296)	(2.839)
Committee Chair	3.689***	21.588*	4.206***
	(.634)	(9.530)	(.601)
Seniority	.001	−.539***	.083*
	(.008)	(.126)	(.035)
Majority	−2.332	13.219	49.615**
	(7.546)	(115.015)	(16.819)
Sex	.125	12.461	−.085
	(.865)	(11.998)	(.523)
Black	−4.365***	−5.321	.073
	(1.246)	(19.010)	(1.088)
Contextual Variables and Interactions			
Legislative Professionalism	−35.793**	106.511^	
	(13.603)	(64.252)	
Term Limits	−8.752	−28.710	−13.475***
	(4.241)	(24.593)	(1.595)
Seniority*Term Limits	.504^	−.900	.921**
	(.294)	(4.481)	(.349)
Leader Tools	−3.261	−16.223	2.061*
	(2.532)	(15.866)	(.979)
Leader Tools* Majority	.638	−8.057	−6.397***
	(.830)	(12.646)	(1.275)
Leader Tools* Leader	−3.093**	25.555	−3.341***
	(1.146)	(17.455)	(.864)
Process Limits	−5.111***	−13.907*	
	(1.424)	(6.406)	
Divided Government	−.755	−14.236	14.994***
	(3.225)	(18.328)	(2.349)
Divided Government* Majority	1.182	29.993	−5.542*
	(1.489)	(22.681)	(2.669)
Majority Size	−.339	−.955	1.228***
	(.264)	(1.497)	(.188)
Majority Size*Majority	.019	.152	−.455*
	(.101)	(1.533)	(.203)

continued

Table 3.4 continued

	Lead Sponsorship	Co–Sponsorship	Amendment Sponsorship
Democratic Control	4.396^	15.137	
	(2.466)	(14.967)	
Black*Democratic Control	6.666**	−86.165**	
	(2.060)	(31.326)	
Sex*Democratic Control	−1.748	−4.760	
	(1.142)	(12.967)	
Pennsylvania Dummy		312.452***	
		(21.836)	
Constant	51.755	146.061	−83.520
−2 Log likelihood	−3854.49***	−6773.24***	−1703.08***
Level 1 N	1095	1095	554
Level 2 N	10	10	6

Note: ^ p < .10, * p < .05, ** p < .01, *** p < .001

Furthermore, majority party status is not significantly related to lead or co-sponsorship levels, which is surprising given the consistency of past research, although majority party members are considerably more active in sponsoring amendments. Of course, this individual level relationship is conditioned by context, so it is not accurate to say that majority party does not matter. Instead, the relationship of majority party status to activity is conditioned by the context in which legislating takes place, as important effect missed by past research. Sex and race are generally unrelated to activity levels with one exception: black legislators are less active in lead sponsoring bills.

This analysis shows, though, that there is an important caveat here: almost all of these findings are conditioned by the effect of contextual variables. So for instance, the legislative activity of party leaders is conditioned by the amount of tools they have as the significant interaction in Table 3.4 shows. Party leaders with the least amount of tools, on the left of Figure 3.2, have legislative behavior that is most distinct from their non-leader counterparts, while party leaders that have the most tools are less distinctive.[4] So, for example, a party leader in Wyoming, which gives its party leaders the least power among these states, would be expected to sponsor approximately 6 (5.7) more bills than a non-party leader, while a party leader in Indiana would be expected to sponsor 1.5 fewer bills than a non-party leader. The Wyoming party leader would co-sponsor approximately 57 fewer bills than the Indiana

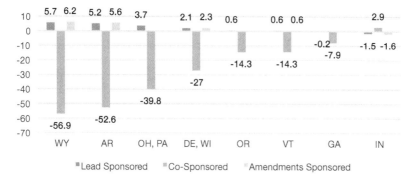

Figure 3.2 The Activity of Party Leaders vs. Non-Party Leaders, based on Leader Tools

leader though, who is predicted to co-sponsor about three more bills as Figure 3.2 shows. So, while the leader tools variable is not significant on its own in the lead and co-sponsorship models and the effect size is small in the amendments model, this variable is still important to understanding the activity levels of party leaders in these chambers. Importantly, leaders with the most tools have behavior that is least distinctive, while leaders with the least tools have behavior that is most distinctive. In the absence of other resources to help alleviate the demands of running an institution, party leaders with few tools allocate their time differently than those who can rely on those formal tools.

Next, seniority is positively related to amendment sponsorship, but it is negatively related to co-sponsorship; the relationship between seniority and lead sponsorship is minute and not significant. This effect confirms what has been found in more recent research, in that more senior legislators co-sponsor fewer bills than their less senior counterparts. It appears that more senior legislators are devoting more of their time to activities other than co-sponsorship, perhaps seeing this as a less efficient way to achieve their goals. As one legislative aide recently noted, "not a lot of meat is expected of freshman representatives, but there are plenty of opportunities to co-sponsor bills."[5] This confirms past research, which suggests those who are less privileged are more likely to turn to co-sponsorship.

Importantly though, the effect of this variable is conditioned by the presence of term limits as shown in Table 3.5. Generally speaking, term limits serve to amplify the effect of seniority, as hypothesized in Chapter 2. While the coefficient for seniority in term limited states is not significant in the co-sponsorship model, it is significant in the lead and amendment sponsorship models, demonstrating that term limits affect the initiation of

Table 3.5 Seniority Simple Slopes, Controlling for the Presence of Term Limits

	Lead Sponsorship	Amendment Sponsorship
No Limits	.001	.083*
	(.008)	(.035)
Term Limited	.504^	1.005**
	(.294)	(.348)

Note: ^ p < .10, * p < .05, ** p < .01, *** p < .001

legislation by legislators serving in these chambers. So, a legislator starting his or her first term in a term limited state would sponsor approximately six fewer amendments than a legislator who had served three terms (or six years).[6] The same difference in experience in a non-term limited state would produce only a half of an additional amendment. It would take a legislator in a non-term limited state over 12 years to achieve the same increase in activity as a legislator in a term limited state. Miquel and Snyder (2006) suggest that legislating is learning by doing; these results suggest that term limits accelerate this learning when it comes to taking the lead in legislating.

Majority party status, on its own, only has a significant effect for proposing amendments; majority party members propose more amendments than minority party members. But the effect of majority party status is difficult to disentangle, as this variable is also conditioned by several chamber level variables.[7] Figure 3.3 shows the overall effect of majority party on amendment sponsorship, incorporating the effect of these interactive relationships. For each state, state values for leader tools, divided government, and majority size were entered, such that the effect shown in Figure 3.3 represents the difference between majority and minority party members in sponsoring amendments in these chambers. As the results show, majority party members sponsor more amendments in each chamber, but the effect size is markedly different across chamber, based on political conditions and resources. In Wyoming, majority party members sponsor over 11 more amendments, while in Indiana, the difference is less than one amendment.

Gender is not significant in any of these models, confirming past research that suggests when other explanatory variables, like seniority and majority status, are accounted for, gender differences in activity are minimal. On its own, the effect of race on activity is negative for lead and co-sponsorship, although this variable is only significant in the lead sponsorship model. However, the effects of both of these individual level variables are, like so many of the other variables, conditioned by chamber level variables. For instance, Democratic control of the legislature dampens the negative effect

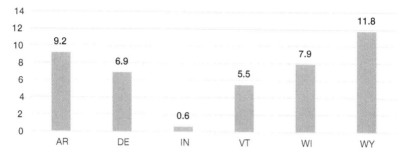

Figure 3.3 Amendment Sponsorship of Majority Party Members, based on Leader
Tools, Divided Government and Majority Size

Table 3.6 Simple Slopes, Controlling for Partisan Control of the Legislature

	Black Lead	Black Co	Women Lead
Republican	–4.353***	–5.322	.125
	(1.248)	(19.042)	(.865)
Democratic	2.302	–91.487**	–1.623*
	(1.627)	(24.731)	(.806)

Note: ^ p < .10, * p < .05, ** p < .01, *** p < .001

of race on activity, even after controlling for the effect of majority party
status. For example, in Republican controlled chambers, black legislators
serve as lead sponsors on approximately four fewer bills than their white
counterparts, while in Democratic controlled legislatures, their lead sponsorship activity is not significantly different than their white counterparts, as
Table 3.6 shows. However, women in Democratic chambers lead sponsor
significantly fewer bills than their male counterparts, while their behavior
is no different in Republican chamber.

Interestingly, black legislators are less active as co-sponsors of bills in
Democratic chambers, by large margins, suggesting that in these chambers,
black legislators shift their time from co-sponsorship activity to focus on
lead sponsorship. The effect here is particularly large, with black legislators
co-sponsoring over 90 fewer bills than their white counterparts in Democratic
chambers. The size of this effect seems to be driven primarily by large
differences in co-sponsorship rates in Pennsylvania (even though there is a
dummy variable for this in the model), where white legislators co-sponsor
475 bills on average, while black legislators co-sponsor 273 bills on average.[8]

However, the black Democratic control variable remains significant in the lead sponsor model, even allowing for the black slope to vary across states. Given that the Democrats are generally more amenable to the policy concerns of African Americans, it is not surprising that these legislators are more active in sponsoring bills in these conditions as they should be more likely to succeed in these conditions. The negative effect of Democratic control on the lead sponsorship activities on female legislators is surprising though, as the rationale is similar for black legislators.

In looking at the chamber level variables, it is clear that for many of these variables, their important effects are both direct and indirect. All of these variables are significant on their own in at least one model. But importantly they also condition the effect of individual resources and networks. Indeed, the two chamber level variables without interaction effects are significant on their own: legislative professionalism and process limits. Some past research has shown that legislative activity is enhanced in more professional chambers. But while co-sponsorship activity is higher in more professional chambers, this relationship is not significant. Interestingly, lead sponsorship is diminished in more professional chambers, suggesting that legislators are focusing their additional resources on other activities, like constituency service and oversight.

Finally, as hypothesized, process limits have a consistently negative effect on lead and co-sponsorship levels. For each additional limit on the legislative process, legislators lead sponsor five fewer bills and co-sponsor close to 15 fewer bills. Thus, these results suggest these limits serve to reduce

Table 3.7 Modeling the Effect of Individual Process Limits

	Lead Sponsorship	Co-Sponsorship		
Limited Introductions	−2.928 (2.431)			
Introduction Deadline	−13.619*** (1.508)	−44.014* (18.319)		
Signature Limits			−31.854 (23.178)	
Co–Sponsor Deadline				−100.588^ (58.201)
−2 Log likelihood	−3848.01***	−6771.61***	−6772.83***	−6771.98***
Level 1 N	1095	1095	1095	1095
Level 2 N	10	10	10	10

Note: $^\wedge$ p < .10, * p < .05, ** p < .01, *** p < .001

the number of bills introduced, allowing legislators to give greater scrutiny to individual pieces of legislation. This leads to the question of which of these process limits is driving these effects. Due to the number of states and the number of other state level variables, it was not possible to run a model with a dummy variable for each process limit. So instead, the models in Table 3.4 were re-run with individual limits substituted in place of the summative variable; the results are show in Table 3.7.[9] This table suggests that the effects, for both lead sponsorship and co-sponsorship, are primarily driven by deadlines. Limits on introductions do not significantly affect lead sponsorship, nor do signature limits for co-sponsorship, although the effect for both is in the expected direction. This makes sense. If legislating is a costly activity, in that legislators have limited amounts of time in the day, and legislators must make decisions about how to allocate their time to a variety of activities, limits that force legislators to condense their law-making activity in to a shorter time frame should have the largest effect, and they do.

Conclusion

Past research on initiating legislation typically focuses on the characteristics, resources and networks of individual legislators and generally finds that these factors shape who initiates legislation and how frequently they do this. But this analysis demonstrates an important caveat to these findings: how these individual level variables affect the initiation of legislation is conditioned by the milieu in which legislating takes place. Additionally, the effect of all of these variables, individual and institutional, vary across different types of legislative activity. For example, party leaders sponsor more bills and amendments. But for less costly activities, like co-sponsorship, resources matter less, and party leaders are less active; they appear to be finding time to lead by taking this time from co-sponsorship activity.

Furthermore, these relationships are conditioned by political conditions and institutional rules and resources. Political conditions, such as divided government, party control of the chamber, and majority size, all have significant effects in shaping how legislators allocate time and effort in legislating. Institutional rules and resources matter too. The tools available to party leaders amplify these effects, such that party leaders with fewer tools are more active lead and amendment sponsors and less active as co-sponsors as compared to their counterparts other chambers with more tools. When leaders have fewer tools, they must use legislation to shape the process and achieve collective goals. But when they have more tools, their legislative behavior is less distinct as they have other mechanisms for achieving collective goals.

Other rules and resources, such as term limits, legislative professionalism and process limits matter too. For instance, process limits tamp down lead and co-sponsorship activity. Deadlines are particularly important in driving this relationship, by condensing the amount of time legislators have to accomplish legislative goals. Limits, then, serve their purpose; they reduce the number of proposals in the pipeline, allowing legislators more time to scrutinize proposals that do come forward. These contextual variables also influence legislative success, as Chapter 5 will show. But before moving on to considering the effects of institutional setting on the outcomes of these proposals, it is worth considering how these variables shape the next stage of the legislative process: committee consideration.

Notes

1 Oregon and Ohio allow for multiple lead sponsors; here, each legislator listed as a lead sponsor is given credit for this lead sponsorship.
2 The variance partition coefficient measures percent of variance explained at the higher level (in this case, state) in a multilevel model. It is calculated per Leckie (2010).
3 All of the models are generally the same with a few exceptions. Due to the fact that co-sponsorship levels in Pennsylvania were drastically different than in other states, the co-sponsorship models were run with a dummy variable for this state and without. The results were generally similar, but the inclusion of the dummy reduced the effect size for some of the variable, so that model was included here. Next, because amendment data was only available for six states, the number of state level variables had to be reduced. While it would have been theoretically preferable to include all variables, that is not possible here. As such, two state level variables were dropped. Process limits were dropped because none of these limits were applicable to amendment activity; they all limited main bills. Additionally, legislative professionalism was dropped as it had the weakest correlation with amendment activity. In alternative specifications where other state variables were dropped, legislative professionalism was never significant, so it was omitted from the model.
4 Standard errors for interaction variables are recalculated per Brambor, Clark, and Golder (2006). Recalculated standard errors demonstrate that these differences are statistically significant (S.E. = 2.591, p < .01 for lead sponsorship; S.E. = 39.495, p < .05 for co-sponsorship; S.E. = 2.018, p < .001 for amendment sponsorship).
5 Personal interview.
6 Simple slopes for interactive variables calculated following the method outlined in Preacher, Curran, and Bauer (2006). For example, in looking at amendment sponsorship, the seniority slope in non-term limited states is .083, while the slope for seniority in term limited states is 1.010, as shown in Table 3.5.
7 None of the interactions with majority party status are significant for the lead sponsorship or co-sponsorship models, but the amount of leader tools (S.E. = 15.685, p <.01), divided government (S.E. = 14.489, p <.01) and majority size

(S.E. = 16.618, p < .01) all condition this relationship for amendment sponsorship (recalculated standard errors and significance levels for interactions reported in parentheses).

8   Indeed, if the co-sponsorship model is run again, allowing the slope of the black variable to vary by state, then the black Democratic interaction variable, while still large and negative (-35.227) is no longer significant. The effect of the other variables in this model remains the same in terms of significance, magnitude, and direction of the significant relationships.

9   Although Table 3.7 does not show the coefficients for the other variables in the mode, the results are generally speaking remain the same. For co-sponsorship, a few variables change from just significant at the .10 level to not significant at the .10 level or vice versa. The only real difference is that the leader tools variable becomes significant in the lead sponsorship model, but the other variables do not change in that model.

References

Anzia, Sarah F. and Molly C. Jackman. 2013. "Legislative Organization and the Second Face of Power: Evidence from U.S. State Legislatures." *Journal of Politics* 75: 210–224.

Binder, Sarah A. 2003. *Stalemate: Causes and Consequences of Legislative Gridlock.* Washington, DC: Brookings Institution Press.

Brambor, Thomas, William Roberts Clark, and Matt Golder. 2006. "Understanding Interaction Models: Improving Empirical Analysis." *Political Analysis* 14: 63–82.

Clucas, Richard C. 2003. "Improving the Harvest of State Legislative Research." *State Politics & Policy Quarterly* 3: 387–419.

Coleman, John J. 1999. "Unified Government, Divided Government, and Party Responsiveness." *American Political Science Review* 93: 821–835.

Frantzich, Stephen. 1979. "Who Makes Our Laws? The Legislative Effectiveness of Members of the U.S. Congress." *Legislative Studies Quarterly* 4: 409–428.

Garand, James C. and Kelly M. Burke. 2006. "Legislative Activity and the 1994 Republican Takeover: Exploring Changing Patterns of Sponsorship and Co-sponsorship in the U.S. House." *American Politics Research* 34: 159–188.

Gray, Virginia and David Lowery. 1995. "Interest Representation and Democratic Gridlock." *Legislative Studies Quarterly* 20 (4): 531–552.

Highton, Benjamin and Michael S. Rocca. 2005. "Beyond the Roll Call Arena: The Determinants of Position Taking in Congress." *Political Research Quarterly* 58: 303–316.

Kessler, Daniel and Keith Krehbiel. 1996. "Dynamics of Co-sponsorship." *American Political Science Review* 90: 555–566.

Kirkland, Justin H. 2011. "The Relational Determinants of Legislative Outcomes: Strong and Weak Ties Between Legislators." *Journal of Politics* 73 (3): 887–898.

Kousser, Thad. 2010. "Does Party Polarization Lead to Policy Gridlock in California?" *California Journal of Politics and Policy* 2 (2): 1–2.

Krehbiel, Keith. 1995. "Co-sponsors and Wafflers from A to Z." *American Journal of Political Science* 39: 906–923.

Krutz, Glen S. 2005. "Issues and Institutions: 'Winnowing' in the U.S. Congress." *American Journal of Political Science* 49: 313–326.

Leckie, George. 2010. Center for Multilevel Modeling. Accessed at www.bristol. ac.uk/media-library/sites/cmm/migrated/documents/7-practicals-stata-sample.pdf on January 15, 2016.

Miquel, Gerard Padro I. and James M. Snyder. 2006. "Legislative Effectiveness and Legislative Careers." *Legislative Studies Quarterly* 31: 347–381.

National Conference of State Legislatures (NCSL). 1996. Accessed at www.ncsl.org/ documents/legismgt/ILP/96Tab3Pt1.pdf on October 23, 2015.

Platt, Matthew. 2008. "Legislative Problem-Solving: Exploring Bill Sponsorship in Post-War America." Accessed at www.people.fas.harvard.edu/~mplatt/ Documents/Bill%20Introduction%20Paper.pdf on June 4, 2014.

Preacher, Kristopher J., Patrick J. Curran, and Daniel J. Bauer. 2006. "Computational Tools for Probing Interactions in Multiple Linear Regression, Multilevel Modeling, and Latent Curve Analysis. " *Journal of Educational and Behavioral Statistics* 31: 437–448.

Rogers, James R. 2002. "Free Riding in State Legislatures." *Public Choice* 113 (1–2): 59–76.

Rosenthal, Alan. 2004. *Heavy Lifting: the Job of the American Legislature.* Washington, DC: CQ Press.

———. 2008. *Engines of Democracy: Politics and Policymaking in State Legislatures.* Washington, DC: CQ Press.

Schiller, Wendy J. 1995. "Senators as Political Entrepreneurs: Using Bill Sponsorship to Shape Legislative Agendas." *American Journal of Political Science* 39 (1): 186–203.

Squire, Peverill. 1998. "Membership Turnover and the Efficient Processing of Legislation." *Legislative Studies Quarterly* 32 (1): 23–32.

———. 2007. "Measuring Legislative Professionalism: The Squire Index Revisited." *State Politics and Policy Quarterly* 7: 211–227.

4 Committee Processing

Once a bill is introduced, it is almost always referred to committees in all U.S. legislatures. Committees are typically empowered to review, alter, and even kill these bills. But there is considerable variation in whether or not these bills are actually reported out of committee. For instance, the Appropriations Committee in Pennsylvania reported out almost 58 percent of the bills that came through that committee, whereas the Appropriations Committee in Georgia reported out only about one-third of the bills it received. The Wyoming Education Committee looked fairly favorably on the 51 bills that crossed its path, reporting out over 77 percent of them; legislators on the Oregon Education Committee looked far less favorably on the 126 bills that it received, reporting out about 34 percent of them, for a report rate of about half that of the Wyoming Education Committee. In Vermont, the Education Committee was even stingier, as it only reported out a little over 13 percent of the 69 bills it received.

Clearly then, there is considerable variation in the activities of committees in state legislatures. However, little is known about why these work patterns vary, despite the fact that committees emerged as important actors in state legislatures as early as the second half of the nineteenth century (Squire 2012, 261) and remain, to this day, important actors in U.S. state legislatures. Part of the challenge is that the power of committees varies from state to state, ranging from negligible to very important (Hamm, Hedlund and Martorano 2006; Squire 2012; Squire and Hamm 2005, 109; Squire and Moncrief 2010), which makes it difficult to study their role in the legislative process. But given that there is reason to believe that committees play very different roles in legislative institutions, it is worthwhile to attempt to overcome these difficulties.

As noted in Chapter 2, there is a good deal of research on the composition of these committees, focusing on the prevalence of outlier committees and the distribution of preferences on committees as compared to the parent chamber (Battista 2004; Hedlund and Hamm 1996; Overby and Kazee 2000;

Overby, Kazee, and Prince 2004; Prince and Overby 2005; Richman 2008), variation in the power of committees in state legislatures (Hamm, Hedlund, and Martorano 2006; Hedlund and Hamm 1996; Martorano 2006), and issues such as when and under what circumstances legislative institutions will choose different committee arrangements (Battista 2009; Martorano 2006; Richman 2008). But there is little research examining variations in the patterns of committee activity within and across legislatures. It may be that some committees are more active in sponsoring and processing legislation, while others may be more passive. For instance, legislators who are more active or entrepreneurial tend to be more successful (Anderson et al. 2003; Rundquist and Strom 1987), but it is not clear whether committees themselves can be more active or entrepreneurial. To be sure, committees are really collections of individuals who possess these traits that come together to make decisions, but it may also be true that the actions of the whole are different than the sum of the parts.

Some committees may report most of the legislation referred, while others may kill the majority of these bills. Some committees may actively engage in putting forward their own legislative proposals, while others may not be empowered to act in this manner. Given that passage rates vary fairly dramatically in the states (ranging from three percent in Minnesota to 73 precent in Arkansas), it is useful to consider the role of committees in explaining some of this variation and in better understanding the legislative process generally. Furthermore, given the important role of context in shaping the work of actors within legislatures, examining how institutional rules, resources and political conditions facilitate or undermine a more active role for committees in the legislative process is critical.

Committees in the States

No two state legislatures in the U.S. have legislative committee systems that are exactly the same, so it is useful to start with some description of the committee systems in the states under examination here. Comparative analyses of committee power shows variation in the independence and rights of committees in state legislatures (Hamm, Hedlund, and Martorano 2006; Martorano 2006), which, as these authors note, make it difficult to fully assess their role in the legislative process. This is true for the states under examination here, as Table 4.1 shows. The number of committees in these states varies from a low of 10 committees (all of which are joint committees with the Senate) in Wyoming to a high of 39 committees in Wisconsin.[1] While it may seem logical that larger chambers will have more committees, this is not necessarily the case here. For instance, the number

Table 4.1 State Committee Systems

State	Chamber Size	Number of Committees	Committee Members (Average and Standard Deviation)	Committee Partisan Balance (Average and Standard Deviation)	Chamber Party Balance
Arkansas	100	16	22.75 9.41	76.31 9.39	75.00
Delaware	41	25	10.00 3.36	60.96 7.10	53.66
Georgia	180	34	19.18 13.41	63.17 9.42	58.89
Indiana	100	23	12.48 2.76	56.71 3.08	51.00
Ohio	99	20	18.30 5.87	52.91 1.97	52.53
Oregon	60	18	8.11 3.69	57.72 1.93	51.67
Pennsylvania	203	27	27.93 4.88	55.28 1.33	50.25
Vermont	150	14	11.00 0.00	61.81 6.38	62.00
Wisconsin	99	39	9.84 1.89	58.31 4.11	51.51
Wyoming	60	10	8.80 .63	70.41 5.244	71.67

of committees in the states with 99–100 members ranges from 16 in Arkansas to 39 in Wisconsin.[2]

Not only does the number of committees vary, the size and composition of these committees varies as well.[3] In Vermont, all committees have 11 members—period. Near the other end of the range in committee size is Georgia, which averages 19 members per committee, but the standard deviation in this measure is over 13 members. This is due in large part to the Appropriations Committee, which has 74 members, the largest committee in these states. In Indiana, all committees have 12 members, 7 of whom are from the majority party, with the exception of the Rules and Ways and Means Committees, which have 10 and 25 members respectively. Still, the party balance on these two committees varies only slightly from the party balance on the other committees (60 percent versus 58.3 percent for the others). Pennsylvania also has fairly consistent committee sizes; only the Appropriations, Committee on Committees, and Ethics vary from the standard 29 member committee size, and the latter two committees do not process legislation.

But unlike Indiana, these committees are also different in terms of partisan composition. Both the Appropriations Committee and Committee on Committees have 60 percent or more majority party members, in a chamber where the majority party only controlled 50.25 percent of the seats. Pennsylvania's committee system, then, seems to be primed for majority party control, particularly important when the majority has such a slim margin in the chamber. The majority party controls the Committee on Committees and the Appropriations Committee, and of the 703 bills that were eventually passed by the chamber, only 203 did not pass through the latter, stacked committee. Conversely, in other states, like Oregon, there is far less variation in the partisan composition of these committees. The Oregon clerk notes this is because the rules in the chamber require proportional party balance on committees; this, of course, points to the importance of context in influencing how committees operate. In some chambers, majority parties can stack committee, while in other chambers; they cannot, regardless of their wishes.

Somewhat surprisingly, there is even some variation in the distribution of leadership roles on committees across these states. While majority party committee chairs seem to be the norm in both Congress and most state legislatures, in both Arkansas and Vermont, more than one committee was chaired by a minority party member. In Arkansas, minority party members chaired four committees (representing a quarter of all committees in this chamber), including the Revenue and Taxation and Education Committees. And this is common practice in this chamber according to the House Parliamentarian. Minority party members chaired the Agriculture and

Transportation Committees in Vermont, approximately 15 percent of all committees in that chamber. Thus, in these two chambers, minority party members are not relegated to chairing unimportant committees. Rather, they are assigned to positions of some degree of importance, something that is almost unheard of in this day and age in Congress.

Contextual Effects on Committee Activity

Thus, there is variation in the number, size, partisan balance and even leadership of committees in these states, factors which may shape the role these committees play in the process. But of course, some of this variation may be due to institutional arrangements; for instance, chambers have different rules that restrict or facilitate the role of committees in the legislative process. As Chapter 3 demonstrated, the context in which decision-making occurs can plan an important role in shaping the behavior of actors in these chambers, by raising or lowering the costs of their actions. As such, it is reasonable to expect that committees can play a variety of roles in the legislative process, from sponsoring bills to amending bills to reporting them out of committee.[4]

Following from Chapter 2, there are two main categories of contextual variables that may influence the role that committees play in the legislative process: those related to political parties and partisan control of the chamber and those related to institutional rules and resources. Once again, the margin of party control of the chamber along with the presence of divided government are the political conditions that should have the greatest impact on the work of committees. Smaller margins of control and opposition control of other institutions of government make it more difficult for the majority party to achieve their goals, increasing the costs of action. As such, political parties may seek to use committees as a means to control legislative outputs. Chapter 3 demonstrated the interactive effects of political conditions on legislative activity, so it also seems that the key effect of these variables will be interactive. That is, when parties have lower margins of control and are faced with divided government, parties should have greater incentive to refer bills to specific committees, particularly those where the party has the most power. If this is the case, then these stacked committees should see a lower report rate as committee members work to defend party interests, particularly in chambers where margins are smaller and divided government exists.

Institutional resources and rules should play a role here too, as they did in Chapter 3. Generally speaking, more resources and rules that empower these actors should reduce the costs of action, although how these resources and rules affect what committees do should differ. Legislative professionalism was negatively and significantly related to bill introductions, as were term limits. The former effect is a bit counter-intuitive; more resources should lead to more activity, but it appears instead that with more time and resources, legislators are more strategic in their allocation of time and effort. That may also be true of committees—the additional time may be used to give greater scrutiny of individual proposals, leading to lower report rates. Alternatively, the bills that do make it into the pipeline may be more likely to pass, as legislators devote more time and effort to fewer bills, so there may be a positive relationship.

While term limits reduce expertise and knowledge about the process and so appear to increase the costs of action, there are similar reasons to believe term limits may have either a positive or negative impact on the report rates of these committees. The lack of experience that comes with these limits could lead to greater deference to legislative proposals of others, or to greater willingness to kill these bills, due to less developed legislative networks.

Finally, institutional rules should matter too, just as they did in Chapter 3. Here, the powers of committee are of interest. Rules that give more power to these committees should reduce the cost of action. Chambers that empower committees should see lower report rates overall, as presumably this is why they give these bodies more power and discretion. Of course, the ultimate expression of the effects of institutional rules on the actions of committees is whether these chambers allow committees to engage in bill sponsorship, an issue examined next.

Committees as Sponsors

Before examining report rates, it is worth taking a brief detour to look at the role of committees themselves as sponsors of bills as one of the most fundamental of institutional rules that shape the role of committee in the legislative process is whether chambers allow committees themselves to sponsor bills. Just over 60 percent of all state legislatures allow their committees to sponsor bills (Hamm, Hedlund, and Martorano 2006); five of the states in this sample of states allow committees to initiate legislation.

As state legislatures establish different committees systems, with varying numbers of committees along with varying jurisdictions, comparing committees across states can be difficult. As a result, in order to facilitate comparison amongst these committees across these chambers, committees that commonly occur across these states and that have similar jurisdictions were identified: Agriculture (10), Appropriations (6), Education (10), Health (9), Judiciary (10), Rules (6), Transportation (9), and Ways and Means (10). Not all of these committees occur in each state, but each of these types occurs in at least six states, as is indicated by the number in parentheses following each type. Unsurprisingly, there are decidedly different patterns of committee sponsorship in these chambers. For instance, in Arkansas, the only committee that sponsored bills was the Appropriations Committee, which sponsored 193 bills, a little over 10 percent of all bills introduced in that chamber. Chamber rules in the Arkansas House require that committees must vote unanimously in order to act as a sponsor of legislation; clearly, this does not happen very often (if at all) outside of the Appropriations committee. It may be that it is easier to come to some agreement when money needs to be spent. One legislator may want to spend more than another, but if money must be appropriated, then hashing out some middle ground may be easier than coming to agreement on a substantive issue where action is not required.

In Wisconsin though, most of the 49 bills sponsored by committee came from committees that were not standing committees in the House. The House clerk's office indicates that this is traditionally the case—committees almost never serve as sponsors of bills. The Joint Legislative Council was sponsor for 22 of these bills, and 15 came from the Law Revision Committee. The former committee's primary responsibility is to establish committees to review important issues identified by the legislature (WLC ND). These committees are comprised both of legislators and citizens; they may recommend legislation to the Joint Legislative Council. If a majority on the council approves, then they serve as sponsor for that piece of legislation. The Law Revision Committee is one of the committees that is appointed by the Joint Legislative Council; it is appointed every odd-numbered session year to review laws that are in need of updating (Wis. Stat. § 13.83). The three other bills came from various joint committees. As such, even though there are five chambers that allow committees to serve as sponsors, there are really only three states, Oregon, Vermont, and Wyoming, where there are multiple committees engaged in sponsorship of bills, making it difficult to systemically examine how context shapes the activity levels of these

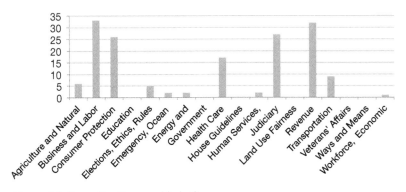

Figure 4.1 Committee Sponsorship in Oregon

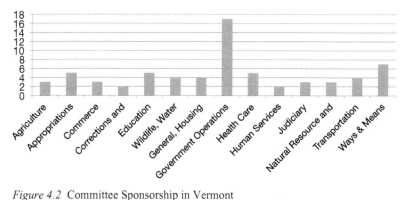

Figure 4.2 Committee Sponsorship in Vermont

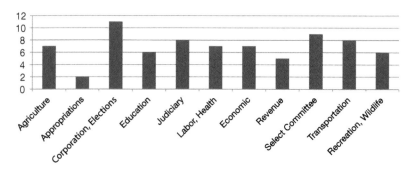

Figure 4.3 Committee Sponsorship in Wyoming

committees. Nonetheless, descriptive analysis shed some light on the patterns of activity in these three chambers. Figures 4.1–4.3 show the distribution of sponsorship in these states.

There does not appear to be clear patterns in the types of committees that sponsor bills in these chambers. Different committees are more active in different states. In Oregon, four committees sponsored more than 20 bills: Business and Labor, Consumer Protection, Judiciary and Revenue. The Oregon clerk's office indicates there are several reasons for having more active committees in this role here. First, while not common, the committee becomes the sponsor of record if a sponsor removes him or herself from the bill. Second, this is also an artifact of having biennial sessions. Committees would work in the interim, studying issues; this work often culminated in committee sponsorship of a bill, after having studied an issue. Oregon has now moved to annual sessions, so it will be interesting to see what impact this has on the role of committees in the legislative process.

In Vermont, no committee sponsored more than 20 bills, but the Government Operations Committee stands out as the most active. Finally, the Corporations and Elections Committee is most active in Wyoming. Add to this the Appropriations Committee in Arkansas, which was the most active there, and the Joint Legislative Council, which was most active in Wisconsin, and it turns out there is no overlap in which committee is most active in these states. Indeed, variables such as committee size and partisan balance on the committee are not significant predictors of committee activity in these states. What does seem clear from these figures, though, is that committee sponsorship of legislation is fairly rare in these chambers, even when they are empowered to act in this role. In only three states (Arkansas, Oregon, and Wisconsin) did any committee sponsor more than 20 bills, and across all five states, there were only five committees out of 97 that sponsored this many bills—that is just over five percent of all the committees in these five states and just over two percent of the 226 committees in the entire sample.

So committees can be more or less active in their introduction of legislation, but the patterns of activity appear to be idiosyncratic to specific chambers. This seems to confirm Squire and Moncrief's (2010, 161) claim that "each legislature has some quirks or oddities that have developed over time and make its process at least a little distinctive," an issue that is covered in more depth in Chapter 6. And despite the fact that the small number of chambers precludes an analysis of the interaction between committee and chamber level variables, there is one important take away with regard to context here. Context clearly matters in that in chambers where rules preclude committees from initiating legislation, they cannot be active in this role. When chambers do allow committees to act in this way, institutional norms shape which committees are active in this role, which highlights the importance of context in shaping the legislative process. In some chambers, such as Arkansas and Wisconsin, only certain committees actually take on this role, while in other chambers, there is more variation.

Committee Report Rates

What is more predictable is the role of committees in reporting legislation in all of these chambers. Ultimately, it is the job of committees to decide on the fate of the bills that come before them. Which will move on and which will die in committee? As expected, the rate at which committees move bills on (their report rates, calculated as the number positively reported out divided by the number introduced times 100) varies across the committees in these chambers and even varies within the chambers. On average, 43.4 percent of the bills referred to these committees are reported out; the standard deviation for this measure is over 24 percent.[5]

Table 4.2 Average Report Rates by State

State	Mean	Standard Deviation
Arkansas	55.18	12.71
Delaware	65.11	26.04
Georgia	45.05	22.71
Indiana	36.91	15.34
Ohio	24.09	16.43
Oregon	44.64	11.27
Pennsylvania	28.12	18.60
Vermont	23.07	16.00
Wisconsin	49.48	24.99
Wyoming	77.29	9.18

Table 4.3 Average Report Rates by Common Committees

Committee	Mean	Standard Deviation
Agriculture	49.66	21.21
Appropriations	58.33	20.54
Education	41.80	21.21
Health	41.60	20.67
Judiciary	44.23	22.08
Transportation	47.58	22.21
Ways and Means	33.63	17.44

Looking at the report rates, Table 4.2 shows there is considerable variation on these measures by state, and these differences are statistically significant at the $p < .001$ level. Vermont has the lowest average report rate; here about 23 percent of all bills reported to committees come out. On the other end of the range is Wyoming where over 77 percent of all bills are reported out of committee. Thus, the range of report rates in these states is over 50 percent. Furthermore, the standard deviation in these report rates does not appear to be related to the average report rate. For example, Wyoming also has the lowest standard deviation, but Delaware, which has the second highest report rate, has the highest standard deviation.

Interestingly, an examination of the difference in report rates across the types of common committees reveals that these differences are NOT statistically significant. As Table 4.3 shows, the range in report rates by committee type (less than 25 percent) is much smaller than the range in report rates by state.

So, patterns in report rates appear to be driven more by state specific factors, rather than common factors that operate across all of these chambers. In other words, context matters in shaping the actions of committees in state legislatures. This is confirmed by examining the likelihood ratio tests, which demonstrate there are significant state effects in the models. These tests reveal that over 38 percent of the variation for report rates is at the state level.[6]

Explaining Committee Reporting Activity

Thus, descriptive analysis demonstrates there is considerable variation in committee activity in these states, and the ratio tests reveal that a good portion of this variation can be attributed to state level factors. So the key question is what state level variables explain these differing patterns of activity. As in Chapter 3, multi-level modeling will be used to predict the committee report rates. As with the previous chapter and as described in Chapter 2, level two in this model will be the legislative chamber, and the contextual variables at this level will include those measuring differences in institutional resources and rules (such as legislative professionalism, term limits, and the rules governing committee processing of legislation) and political conditions (such as divided government and the margin of party control).

In this analysis, level one variables will measure the characteristics of committees. These variables include the size of the committee, whether the committee has a minority party chair, the majority party percent on the committee, and whether the committee is an Appropriations or Ways and Means Committee. Larger committees are expected to have lower report rates, simply because it will be harder to forge agreement on bills as the number of people increases. Minority chair is simply a dummy variable, which indicates if the chair of the committee does not belong to the party that holds the majority in the chamber. The presence of a minority party chair may lead to fewer bills coming out, as the chair would be less inclined to support the interests of the majority party. On the other hand, the chair may better at brokering compromises between party factions, leading to higher report rates.

Because the margin of party control varies from chamber to chamber, the majority party variable is measured as the deviation of any given committee from the average for all committees in the chamber, as noted previously. So, for example, the average committee in Ohio is 53 percent Republican, and the standard deviation in that chamber is approximately two percent around this average; a committee with a 58 percent Republican majority might be seen as stacked. But in Wisconsin, a committee that is 58 percent Republican is right at the chamber and committee average, so it is important to account for these differences. Expectations about the relationship between this variable and report rates are also not clear. Committees with more majority party members may report more bills simply because they have the power to do as they wish; on the other hand, majority party leaders may refer bills that do not reflect the interests of the majority party to stacked committees so they may kill them. So while stacking committees is rare, when it does occur, it may play a strong role in shaping committee activity. Indeed, this is probably what party leaders had in mind when stacking the committee. Interviews with the Oregon clerk's office indicates that party leaders, whether stacking committees or not, think very carefully about who they select for these roles. In this chamber, chairs are very powerful; bills may not be amended on the floor, so all of this work is done in committee. The speaker considers not only seniority but also knowledge of the subject area and party loyalty in making these appointments. The Wisconsin clerk confirmed this is also the case in the state house there; party leaders think carefully about who to place in which committee chair position (starting in the 1980s, an institutional norm developed that all majority party legislators the their second term or beyond are given a committee chair position), and they think carefully about where to send bills, given these norms and decisions.

Finally, Squire and Hamm (2010, 168) indicate that money bills are "must pass" legislation, so a dummy variable is included for each of the committees that process money bills, namely Appropriations or Ways and Means committees. On the one hand, because money bills are must pass bills, these committees may have higher report rates. On the other hand, to the extent these state legislative committee systems resemble those in Congress, these committees may report out fewer bills as they serve as a locus of party control.

Building on results from Chapter 3 and hypotheses from above, both political and institutional variables should influence committee activity levels here. For committees, additional institutional resources should generally induce greater activity, but it is not theoretically clear whether the lowered costs of activity should lead to higher or lower report rates. For instance, the resources that come with professionalization may lead to more time to devote to scrutiny of referred bills (so lower report rates) or to more time to devote to securing passage (so higher report rates) Term limits could lead to greater deference to legislative proposals of others or to greater willingness to kill these bills, due to less developed legislative networks.

Next, institutional rules should have an impact as well. With respect to rules, there is little variation in these states in terms of who appoints members to these committees or who selects committee chairs as this power lies with the majority party, typically with the Speaker; this is true for most state houses. For example, the Speaker does not select committee chairs in only nine state houses overall, and even in these cases, procedures allow for the majority party to control the selection of the chair (NCSL 2015).[7] As such, the focus here is on rules that constrain committees' ability to process legislation. The National Conference of State Legislatures and the American Society of State Legislative Clerks and Secretaries (NCSL 1996) identify a variety of rules concerning how committees operate in these state legislatures, but many of these, such as requirements for how committee minutes are delivered to members, do not seem particularly relevant for this analysis. Instead, five key rules that affect committee actions and reports are measured here. These are: who determines which bills will be heard (0 = outside committee; 1 = committee or committee chair); who determines when a bill will be heard (0 = outside committee; 1 = committee or committee chair); whether a committee is required to hear all referred bills (0 = yes; 1 = no); whether a committee has the power to kill or table a bill (0 = no; 1 = yes); and whether a committee is required to provide a report on all bills referred to them (0 = yes; 1 = no).

While at first these codings may seem counter-intuitive, the end result is that committees with the most discretion will have higher scores, and committees with the least discretion will have lower scores. Scores can theoretically range from 0 to 5, but they actually range from 3 (in Arkansas and Ohio) to 5 (in Georgia, Oregon, Pennsylvania, and Vermont), as shown in Table 1.3. This variable is expected to negatively relate to report rates, as committees will have more discretion to act.[8]

Building on the explanations from Chapter 2 and the findings from Chapter 3, political conditions are also expected to have an impact here; conditions that make it more difficult for the majority party to control the process, such as a slim margin of control and divided government, should lead to parties seeking to use committees to exert control over the legislative process, as described earlier. Report rates should be lower when there is a small margin of control and divided government. Additionally, the effect should be more pronounced on those committees that are stacked with majority party members, as noted above. Finally, the number of bills will be included in the model as Squire and Moncrief (2010, 164) note an inverse relationship between the number of bills introduced and the proportion that passes, a finding that may extend to committees.

As Table 4.4 reveals, both individual and contextual variables are only infrequently related to committee report rates for these chambers. However, there are some significant and interesting relationships in these models. At the committee level, larger committees are less likely to report out bills.

For each additional member on a committee, the committee reports out approximately .5 percent fewer bills. Add ten members to a committee, and the report rate declines by 5 percent. Having more members appears to raise the cost of legislating, perhaps by making it more difficult to forge agreement.

In addition, as in Congress, the prestige Appropriations and Ways and Means Committees operate in a significantly different manner than other committees in these chambers. Appropriations Committees are significantly more likely to report out bills; 25 percent more as compared to other committees. This is, generally, a reflection of the way states handle appropriations. Indeed, when controls are added for whether the appropriations process is omnibus or not, the coefficient for the Appropriations committee is significant and positive (45.233, S.E. = 12.254), while the interaction between the Appropriations variable and the process variable is negative (–38.882, S.E. 15.936), although it is no longer significant.[9] Essentially, what this means is that appropriations committees in states with omnibus appropriations bills are no more or less likely than other committees to report out bills. Appropriations Committees in states with multiple appropriations bills report out significantly more than other committees, simply because they have to in order to get a state budget in place. This confirms Squire and Hamm's (2010, 168) assertion that these are must pass bills.

Ways and Means Committees, however, are significantly more likely to kill bills as compared to other committees in these chambers. They report out just over 11 percent fewer bills, indicating that it is more difficult to forge agreement on bills that raise revenue, the traditional jurisdiction of Ways and Means Committees. This is hardly surprising; spending is far more popular than taxing, so it is harder to get people to agree to support these bills. This holds true whether the chamber is controlled by Democrats, who would presumably be more likely to support bills that would increase revenue, or Republicans, who would presumably be more likely to support bills that decrease revenue.[10]

Looking at the contextual variables, few contextual variables are significant. The effects of resources and rules tend to be negative, suggesting that more resources and rules that empower committees as actors leads them to engage in greater scrutiny of the proposals that come before them, although these effects are not statistically significant. Only the interaction between divided government and committee majority percent is statistically significant. This variable captures the effect when there is divided government and the committee majority percent is one standard deviation above the party balance on all committees in the chamber (in other words, it is stacked). The coefficient indicates that stacked committees in divided chambers report out approximately 10 percent fewer bills, indicating that under conditions of divided government, parties seek to use stacked committees to defend party interests.

Table 4.4 Modeling Committee Report Rates

	Percent Reported
Committee Level Variables	
Committee Size	−.419^
	(.228)
Minority Party Chair	−3.038
	(9.224)
Majority Percent	8.798
	(14.231)
Appropriations	25.333**
	(9.136)
Ways and Means	−11.873*
	(5.927)
Contextual Variables and Interactions	
Legislative Professionalism	−71.679
	(79.308)
Term Limits	−5.619
	(27.666)
Committee Power	−6.433
	(8.458)
Divided Government	−.791
	(21.454)
Divided * Committee Majority Percent	−10.723**
	(3.263)
Chamber Majority Party Percent	−.773
	(.897)
Chamber Majority * Committee Majority Percent	−.124
	(.234)
Total Bills	.001
	(.012)
Constant	137.263
−2 Log likelihood	−910.306
Level 1 N	214
Level 2 N	10

Note: ^ $p < .10$, * $p < .05$, ** $p < .01$, *** $p < .001$

Overall then, despite the fact that the ratio tests showed significant state effects, the contextual variables perform poorly in both models. However, that does not necessarily mean that the context in which committee activity occurs is not important. Instead, it seems to support Squire and Hamm's notion about the quirks and oddities of legislating in state legislatures. There are clearly different patterns in how and which committees are active in these chambers, but these patterns are not consistent across chambers.

Conclusion

As the descriptive analysis demonstrated, there are clearly different patterns of committee activity in these states. For example, some chambers, like the Pennsylvania and Wyoming houses, have committee systems where most bills ultimately pass through a committee stacked by majority party members; such chambers seem to have committee systems primed for majority party control. However, the models showed that these patterns of committee activity are not easily predictable, although some generalizations are possible. Prestige matters; committees dealing with money, such as Appropriations and Ways and Means committees, operate differently than other committees in these chambers. The party balance on a committee matters too, particularly under conditions of divided government; committees with more majority party member report out fewer bills under divided government.

And despite the poor performance of contextual variables, the choices legislators make about institution rules matter; rules that empower actors, like rules that allow committees to serve as sponsors, and lower their costs of acting have their intended effects, just as in Chapter 3. This is also not to say that context is not important. Rather, context seems to be highly particular to given institutions, an issue that is discussed in Chapter 6.

Of course, bills that pass out of committee are not through the woods yet as support from the entire chamber is necessary before a bill becomes law. Thus, the final question here is what happens next? What happens to the bills that come out of these committees? Why do some bills move on while others falter? Why are some legislators more successful than others? And how does the context in which these decisions take place matter?

Notes

1 Wyoming does have numerous select committees, with members from the House and Senate as well. However, these committees do not process legislation, although they can propose legislation. These committees are not included in examinations of the processing of legislation in this chapter, but their bill

introductions, which are fairly limited, are grouped together in the discussion of committee sponsorship below.

2 The total number of committees listed here include all standing committee in these chambers. However, some committees in these chambers are not active in processing legislation. That is, they neither received nor reported any legislation during this session. Examples include the House Guidelines Committee in Oregon and the Ethics Committee in Pennsylvania. These committees are not included in the analysis of committee referral and report rates that follows.

3 The majority party variable is measured as the deviation of any given committee from the average for all committees in the chamber.

4 Due to variations in how states report legislative data, it is not possible to examine the amendment activity of committees in these states, but it is possible to examine how context shapes the sponsorship and reporting activity of committees.

5 It is important to note that this does not weight by the number of bills referred each committee (in other words, it counts all committees equally—those receiving and reporting one bill are given equal weight to those receiving 100 bills and reporting one bill). Also, in most cases, bills that are not reported out of committee die in that committee. But in some rare cases, bills are not reported out of committee because they are removed. Bills are removed from committee via a variety of methods in these chambers. It is rare that bills are removed via a discharge petition, although this does sometimes happen; more common is removal by a vote of the committee itself. That is, the committee votes to send the bill to another committee without a report, positive or negative. Because there are varying reasons bills are removed from the committee in these chambers, these bills were not included in numerator or denominator of the report rates for the committee that voted the bill out. These bills were counted for the committee to which the bill was moved. So for instance, if a bill was initially referred to the Education Committee which votes to move it to the Transportation committee, that bill would be counted for the Transportation Committee, but not the Education Committee. Note this is different from multiple referrals as the first committee does not produce a report, either positive or negative, before transferring it to the other committee.

6 Using the same tests from Chapter 3, the overall mean for report rates is 43.966, while the VPC/ICC (which measures the percent of variation at the state level) is 38.690. The log ratio test is 60.306, which is significant at $p < .001$.

7 The state legislative clerk's office was contacted in these chambers to confirm that these selection methods were in place during this session.

8 Despite the fact that one of these variables measures whether committee are required to report bills, as is the case in Wyoming, no state has a report rate of 100 percent, which means that this rule acts as a paper, not an actual, restraint. Nonetheless, this variable should have some impact on committee activity as committees may only act in violation of this rule with good reason. Unfortunately, while there is enough variation across the states to measure the impact of these powers as a scale, there is not enough variation in these powers individually to test the independent impact of each of these powers, as was done in Chapter 3 for leader tools. For three of the powers (which bills heard, when bills heard, and report all), only one state is different than the others, while for the other two

(hear all and kill bill), only two states differ. Fortunately, there tends to be little overlap in which states differ on which measure, but the lack of variation precludes analyzing each power independently.

9 The effect size and significance levels for all other variables remain substantially the same is in Table 4.4. The Recalculated simple slope is 6.351, with a standard error of 12.230.

10 An additional model with an interaction between party control and the Ways and Means variable was run, and this interaction was not significant, nor did it change the other results.

References

Anderson, William D., Janet Box-Steffensmeier, and Valeria Sinclair-Chapman. 2003. "The Keys to Legislative Success in the U.S. House of Representatives." *Legislative Studies Quarterly* 28: 357–386.

Battista, James Coleman. 2004. "Reexamining Legislative Committee Representativeness in the States." *State Politics and Policy Quarterly* 4: 161–180.

———. 2009. "Why Information? Choosing Committee Informativeness in U.S. State Legislatures." *Legislative Studies Quarterly* 34: 375–397.

Hamm, Keith E., Ronald D. Hedlund, and Nancy Martorano. 2006. "Measuring State Legislative Committee Power: Change and Chamber Differences in the 20th Century." *State Politics and Policy Quarterly* 6: 88–111.

Hedlund, Ronald D. and Keith E. Hamm. 1996. "Political Parties as Vehicles for Organizing U.S. State Legislative Committees." *Legislative Studies Quarterly* 21: 383–408.

Martorano, Nancy. 2006. "Balancing Power: Committee System Autonomy and Legislative Organization." *Legislative Studies Quarterly* 31: 205–234.

National Conference of State Legislatures (NCSL). 1996. Accessed at www.ncsl.org/documents/legismgt/ILP/96Tab3Pt1.pdf on October 23, 2015.

———. 2015. Accessed at www.ncsl.org/legislatures-elections/legislatures/the-selection-of-committee-chairs.aspx on October 23, 2015.

Overby, L. Marvin and Thomas A. Kazee. 2000. "Outlying Committees in the Statehouse: An Examination of the Prevalence of Committee Outliers in State Legislatures." *Journal of Politics* 62: 701–728.

Overby, L. Marvin, Thomas A. Kazee, and David W. Prince. 2004. "Committee Outliers in State Legislatures." *Legislative Studies Quarterly* 29: 81–107.

Prince, David W. and L. Marvin Overby. 2005. "Legislative Organization Theory and Committee Preference Outliers in State Senates." *State Politics and Policy Quarterly* 5: 68–87.

Richman, Jesse. 2008. "Uncertainty and the Prevalence of Committee Outliers." *Legislative Studies Quarterly* 33: 323–347.

Rundquist, Barry S. and Gerald S. Strom. 1987. "Bill Construction in Legislative Committees: A Study of the U.S. House." *Legislative Studies Quarterly* 12: 97–113.

Squire, Peverill. 2012. *The Evolution of American Legislatures: Colonies, Territories, and States, 1619–2009.* Ann Arbor, MI: University of Michigan Press.

Squire, Peverill and Keith E. Hamm. 2005. *101 Chambers: Congress, State Legislatures, and the Future of Legislative Studies.* Columbus, OH: Ohio State University Press.

Squire, Peverill and Gary Moncrief. 2010. *State Legislatures Today: Politics Under the Domes.* Boston, MA: Longman.

Wisconsin Legislative Council (WLC). ND. "Wisconsin Legislative Council: Supporting Effective Lawmaking Since 1947." Accessed at http://legis.wisconsin. gov/lc/committees/jointcouncil/ on October 23, 2015.

Wis. Stat. § 13.83. Accessed at http://docs.legis.wisconsin.gov/document/statutes/ 13.83 on October 23, 2015.

5 What Happens Next

In the 2007–2008 session of the Vermont state legislature, House Bill 256 was introduced on February 8, 2007. Of the 150 legislators in the lower chamber, 110 signed on to sponsor the bill, yet the bill died in the Human Services committee, without a single hearing. House Bill 11, on the other hand, was introduced on January 9, 2007; only one representative signed on to sponsor this bill. It was referred to the Education Committee and moved out of committee on March 26, even though it had not garnered more support in the form of additional sponsors. After moving past this crucial step, HB 11 was eventually signed into law. During this session, Republicans controlled the chamber, and over 70 percent of the sponsors for HB 256 were Republican. Numerous sponsors held positions of power in the legislature, as party leaders or committee chairs. On the other hand, the sponsor of HB 11 was a Democrat and was not on the Education Committee or in any position of leadership. Yet HB 11 passed, while HB 256 died.

During the same time frame in Pennsylvania, there were over a dozen bills introduced in the 2007–2008 legislative session that had over 102 sponsors. Yet only one of these bills passed, despite the fact that 102 represents more than half of all legislators in the chamber. In that same chamber though, 98 bills had just one sponsor, and over one-third of those bills passed. In Ohio, less than 20 percent of the bills reported from the Ways and Means Committee passed the House, while just over 50 percent of the bills reported from the Wyoming Ways and Means Committee ultimately passed into the Senate. Conversely, almost 99 percent of the bills reported from the Pennsylvania Appropriations Committee were approved by the full chamber.

As the above examples illustrate, the legislative process is complicated. Understanding why some bills pass and others do not requires looking at this question from multiple viewpoints. A number of studies have examined why passage rates vary within chambers (Krutz 2005) or across the states generally (Bowling and Ferguson 2001; Gray and Lowery 1995; Hicks and

Table 5.1 Percent of Introduced Bills that Passed House

	State
Arkansas	60.1
Delaware	60.3
Georgia	46.5
Indiana	25.0
Ohio	19.5
Oregon	35.1
Pennsylvania	11.9
Vermont	18.3
Wisconsin	26.5
Wyoming	57.0

Note: These differences are statistically significant at $p < .001$

Smith 2009; Squire 1998), but there is little research that examines how within chamber variables interact with chamber level variables to shape the outputs of legislative institutions. And as Table 5.1 shows, there is considerable variation across the states to explain.

What determines the success of individual actors in these chambers and how is their success shaped by the context within which these actions occur? What explains variation in the rate at which committee actions are supported by colleagues in these institutions? And finally, how do these factors come together to shape the ultimate fate of any given bill within a legislative chamber? In other words, what determines success? In order to get at answers to these questions, this chapter looks at legislative outcomes in three different ways. First, following from Chapter 3, it looks at how the individual characteristics of legislators interact with the institutional context to shape legislative success. Second, following from Chapter 4, it looks committee success, by examining variation in the rates at which bills that are approved by committees are supported by the full chamber. Finally, this chapter examines how these factors come together in different contexts to shape passage by the entire chamber. Taken together, these analyses demonstrate the complicated ways that context shapes the actions of actors within these institutions and influences the work product that comes out of them.

Legislative Effectiveness

To start, we can look at what happens next by looking at the effectiveness of individual legislators. Chapter 3 demonstrated that the effect of context on legislating is nuanced; that is, contextual variables have different effects on different types of legislative activity. For instance, party leaders with fewer tools engage in less co-sponsorship and more lead sponsorship as compared to party leaders in other chambers with more tools. So it seems reasonable to assume that context will shape legislative effectiveness, and that the relationship of these contextual variables to success will vary across legislative vehicles, as they raise the costs of certain activities but lower the costs of others.

Even at a purely descriptive level, it is clear that this is true. Obviously, variations in legislative effectiveness closely follow patterns in legislative enactments across the states, demonstrating the importance of chamber level variables, as Table 5.2 shows.[1] But the standard deviations for these measures also show that there is wide variation in patterns of effectiveness within a given chamber. Thus, as with the activity measures, the descriptive statistics show that patterns of effectiveness vary within and across states and vary across types of legislative activity.

Looking at the number of lead sponsored bills passed, the standard deviation across the states is lower for this measure than all of the other measures, as was the case for lead sponsorship. Arkansas and Delaware stand out for high averages; in these states, each legislator was able to secure the passage of close to or over eight bills each. This is a reflection of the high overall passage rate in these states (54 percent and 38 percent respectively), which of course leads to the question as to why these chambers are so different. But passage rates are not always closely related to the number of bills passed. For example, Delaware and Georgia have similar overall passage rates, but legislators in the former chamber pass, on average, 4.5 more bills that legislators in the latter chamber.

Legislators in the other states are less successful in securing passage for bills on which they serve as lead sponsors. In no other state is the average greater than four, and in four of these states, the typical legislator passed less than one lead sponsored bill. However, when viewed as a percentage (the percentage of introduced bills passed), lead sponsorship activity is less distinctive. In fact, in most of these states, legislators are more successful in securing passage of legislation where they serve as lead sponsors as these rates are generally higher than the passage rates for co-sponsored bills. This suggests that legislators take lead sponsorship seriously; when they introduce bills, they are committed to working to see them passed. This is less true for co-sponsorship, which indicates that legislators are less committed to this type of activity. Legislators can sign on without having to commit too much of their limited time. However, this is not true in Indiana, where co-sponsorship success rates are higher than lead sponsorship rates. Of course, Indiana is also a state that limits the number of co-sponsors on bills, making

Table 5.2 Legislative Effectiveness

State	Lead Passed (#)	Co-Sponsored Passed (#)	Amendments Passed (#)	Lead Passed (%)	Co-Sponsored Passed (%)	Amendments Passed (%)
Arkansas	8.64 Avg. 0 Min. 26 Max. 5.74 SD	31.65 Avg. 17 Min. 62 Max. 8.14 SD	7.10 Avg. 0 Min. 29 Max. 6.37 SD	55.29 Avg. 9.09 Min. 100 Max. 19.25 SD	70.22 Avg. 48.84 Min. 84.21 Max. 6.14 SD	98.22 Avg. 66.67 Min. 100 Max. 5.72 SD
Delaware	7.59 Avg. 0 Min. 22 Max. 5.26 SD	24.07 Avg. 1 Min. 36 Max. 8.39 SD	3.61 Avg. 0 Min. 15 Max. 3.96 SD	39.58 Avg. 0 Min. 72.73 Max. 17.64 SD	36.74 Avg. 16.67 Min. 48.28 Max. 7.65 SD	58.31 Avg. 0 Min. 100 Max. 26.80 SD
Georgia	2.99 Avg. 0 Min. 14 Max. 2.96 SD	7.12 Avg. 0 Min. 32 Max. 6.05 SD	UA	39.85 Avg. 0 Min. 100 Max. 29.80 SD	27.30 Avg. 0 Min. 75 Max. 14.98 SD	UA
Indiana	1.13 Avg. 0 Min. 7 Max. 1.51 SD	2.50 Avg. 0 Min. 12 Max. 2.19 SD	1.18 Avg. 0 Min. 6 Max. 1.44 SD	11.90 Avg. 0 Min. 50.00 Max. 14.83 SD	26.65 Avg. 0 Min. 80.00 Max. 19.02 SD	66.38 Avg. 0 Min. 100.00 Max. 40.02 SD
Ohio	.92 Avg. 0 Min. 5 Max. 1.27 SD	10.89 Avg. 0 Min. 26 Max. 6.01 SD	UA	14.21 Avg. 0 Min. 100.00 Max. 22.93 SD	23.23 Avg. 0 Min. 60.00 Max. 12.70 SD	UA

Oregon	3.93 Avg. / 0 Min. / 13 Max. / 3.04 SD	15.07 Avg. / 3 Min. / 29 Max. / 7.49 SD	UA	20.29 Avg. / 0 Min. / 56.25 Max. / 12.78 SD	21.39 Avg. / 7.5 Min. / 42.86 Max. / 8.42 SD	UA
Pennsylvania	.76 Avg. / 0 Min. / 38 Max. / 2.75 SD	22.56 Avg. / 0 Min. / 108 Max. / 16.38 SD	UA	6.15 Avg. / 0 Min. / 100 Max. / 13.02 SD	5.63 Avg. / 0 Min. / 21.28 Max. / 2.46 SD	UA
Vermont	.59 Avg. / 0 Min. / 7 Max. / 1.05 SD	3.45 Avg. / 0 Min. / 7 Max. / 2.44 SD	.52 Avg. / 0 Min. / 6 Max. / .99 SD	2.64 Avg. / 10 Min. / 100 Max. / 22.42 SD	10.48 Avg. / 0 Min. / 31.82 Max. / 6.49 SD	67.27 Avg. / 0 Min. / 100.00 Max. / 41.74 SD
Wisconsin	.91 Avg. / 0 Min. / 7 Max. / 1.36 SD	10.47 Avg. / 0 Min. / 53 Max. / 10.83 SD	2.47 Avg. / 0 Min. / 20 Max. / 3.28 SD	10.14 Avg. / 0 Min. / 75.0 Max. / 14.54 SD	8.78 Avg. / 0 Min. / 16.87 Max. / 3.83 SD	53.47 Avg. / 0 Min. / 100 Max. / 31.59 SD
Wyoming	2.00 Avg. / 0 Min. / 7 Max. / 1.86 SD	5.92 Avg. / 0 Min. / 15 Max. / 3.48 SD	9.68 Avg. / 0 Min. / 53 Max. / 11.10 SD	32.76 Avg. / 0 Min. / 100 Max. / 29.65 SD	33.44 Avg. / 0 Min. / 83.33 Max. / 14.21 SD	61.94 Avg. / 0 Min. / 100 Max. / 22.14 SD

Note: Oregon and Ohio allow for multiple lead sponsors; each legislator listed as a lead sponsor is given credit for this lead sponsorship if the bill passed

legislators think more carefully about who to secure as co-sponsors of their proposals. In essence, this rule seems to raise the cost of co-sponsorship, by making both lead sponsors and potential co-sponsors think more carefully about this activity.

Interestingly, while Pennsylvania clearly stood out as an outlier in terms of the average number of bills legislators co-sponsored, it does not necessarily stand out in terms of the number of co-sponsored bills passed. Legislators, on average, in this state passed a little over 22 of the bills they co-sponsored; legislators in Arkansas and Delaware have higher averages on this measure. This suggests that there is some degree of position-taking associated with signing on to co-sponsor bills in Pennsylvania.

What is clear though is that contextual level variables seem to shape the extent to which legislators engage in co-sponsorship as an act of position-taking. Some institutions, like Pennsylvania and Wisconsin where the co-sponsorship success rate is under ten percent, seem to be more like Congress, where position-taking is the norm. Wisconsin and Pennsylvania are the two most professional legislatures here, so it appears that position-taking via co-sponsorship may be more common in professional legislatures, like these two and in Congress, but in other states with less professional legislatures, like Arkansas, this seems less true, as the average success rate on this measure is over 70 percent.

As Chapter 3 demonstrated, there are markedly different institutional norms about amendment sponsorship. Unsurprisingly, these differing norms about amendments also influence amendment passage rates. For example, in Arkansas, only 11 of the 868 amendments that were proposed were not passed; that means close to 99 percent of all proposed amendments passed. In Arkansas then, it is the job of the lead sponsor to secure the compromise necessary to secure passage of the bill, and the only amendments that are proposed are those for which agreement has already been secured. Position taking via amendment proposals or co-sponsorship does not seem to occur in Arkansas. According to the House Parliamentarian, hostile amendments are rare; instead, amendments are put forward to improve bills and to secure the necessary votes for passage. This is in contrast to Wisconsin, where just over 53 percent of proposed amendments were passed. In Wyoming, while those who do not hold chair or leader positions may propose amendments, they are less successful when they do so. Over 42 percent of the amendments proposed by these legislators did not pass, while only 12.1 percent of amendments proposed by chairs or leaders failed.

Unlike with activity levels, success rates across types of legislative activity are correlated, although perhaps not as strongly as might be expected. For instance, the correlation between lead passage rates and co-sponsored passage rates is .650; the correlation between lead sponsorship success and

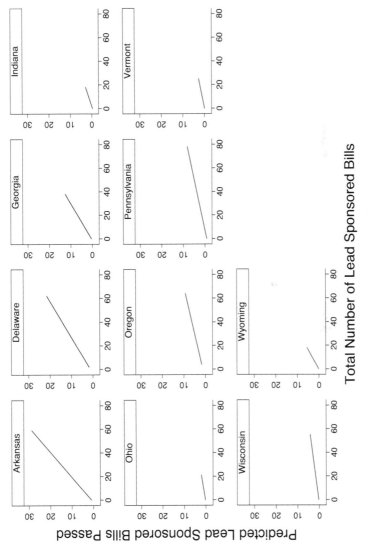

Figure 5.1 Predicted Lead Sponsorship Success, Based on Lead Sponsorship Activity

amendment sponsorship success is .512. The relationship between activity and success varies though. The correlation between amendment sponsorship activity and passage is strongest at .946; across the states, it appears that amendments are vehicles for making things happen as opposed to position taking. Legislators who propose amendments, regardless of whether they are lead sponsors of the bills or chamber leaders, are doing so in order to secure passage of the bill.

On the other end, co-sponsorship activity is significantly, but not over-whelmingly, correlated to co-sponsorship success at .481. Finally, the correlation between lead sponsorship activity and success is correlated at .756. Despite this strong correlation, there is still considerable variation by state in the correlations between sponsorship activity and success rates, outside of amendment activity. For example, Figure 5.1 predicts lead sponsorship success rates based on lead sponsorship activity by state. In some states, like Arkansas, the slope of the line is pronounced, whereas in other states, like Wisconsin, the slope is much flatter. So while there is a positive relationship between activity and success in all of these states, this figure demonstrates the need to examine these relationships in multiple contexts.

Clearly then, there is a good deal of both in state and cross state variation to explain in effectiveness rates. The likelihood ratio tests, as show in Table 5.3, confirm this. They indicate that there are significant state effects in the models across all of the legislative vehicles; this is unsurprising given the variations in patterns of effectiveness seen above. However, as with legislative activity in Chapter 3, these tests also indicate the amount of variance explained by state level factors differs. While Chapter 3 revealed that more of the variance in co-sponsorship activity was due to state level factors as compared to lead sponsorship activity, the portion of variance explained at the state level for passage rates of both lead and co-sponsored bills is very similar, at around 50 percent. However, only about a third of the variation in amendment passage rates is due to state level factors. As with sponsorship rates though, there is considerable variation due to both state and individual level variables across all types of legislative activity, so understanding legislative effectiveness requires models that account for variables at both levels.

Thus, as with Chapter 3, multi-level modeling is appropriate. Contextual variables are expected to have mostly similar effects to those found in Chapter 3. Institutional resources that raise the cost of legislative activity should decrease effectiveness; for instance, legislative process limits should reduce effectiveness. Alternatively, the effect could be the opposite: where the costs of activity are higher, only those proposals most likely to pass may be put forward. The hypothesis here is that the effect will be similar to those

Table 5.3: State Level Variance in Legislative Effectiveness

	Overall mean	*VPC/ICC (% variance at state level)*	*LR*
Lead Passed	2.92	50.03	558.53***
Co Passed	13.36	53.21	729.40***
Amendments Passed	4.08	34.12	167.96***

Note: * p < .05, ** p < .01, > p < .001

found in Chapter 3, although as noted below that may not always be the case. Consistent with that, term limits should also reduce effectiveness, as Chapter 3 demonstrated they reduce initiation. Chapter 3 revealed that divided government reduces the initiation of legislation, but increases the amount of amendments, presumably due to greater need to make proposals more amenable to the branches of government controlled by the other party. Similar effects should occur for effectiveness. Majority size was negatively (but not significantly) related to initiation, confirming the free riding effect; however, it seems that come time to vote, having more majority party members as co-sponsors would be a good thing, so this should be positively related to effectiveness.

Legislative professionalism was negatively related to lead sponsorship in Chapter 3, suggesting that legislators are devoting time to other activities, although it was positively related to co-sponsorship. A similar effect is expected for lead sponsorship here; the time and resources that come with professionalism may lead to greater scrutiny of bills, leading to lower passage rates. The hypothesized effect on co-sponsorship is less clear though; it could be that legislators in more professional chambers are more successful due to having stronger networks; although it may be that the increased co-sponsorship associated with professionalism is related to position taking, leading to decreased effectiveness. Process limits should also serve to reduce effectiveness levels, although it may be with fewer bills in the pipeline, those that remain are stronger and therefore more likely to pass, leading to a positive relationship.

Of course, it is also expected that these contextual variables will have interactive effects; if these variables raise (or lower) the cost of legislating, then they will not do so equally for all legislators. For instance, term limits may serve to amplify the effects of seniority, and party related variables may alter the behavior of majority party members in particular. The effect of leader tools should operate primarily through cross-level interactions, as majority party members empower party leaders to help them accomplish party business (Anzia and Jackman 2013).[2]

The legislator characteristic variables that are included are: party leader, committee chair, seniority, majority party, sex, and black. As in Chapter 3, the same chamber level variables are included, corresponding with the party and institutional factors identified in Chapter 2. The party related variables are party control, margin of party control, and divided government. The institutional variables are legislative professionalism, term limits, process limits, and leader tools.

The multi-level models confirm that different sets of factors are important for explaining different types of legislative activity as was shown in Chapter 3. In all of the models in Table 5.4, individual level variables are significantly related to legislative success, but these relationships are conditioned by institutional variables. Additionally, success is positively and significantly related to activity levels in all three models, although, not surprisingly, the magnitude of this effect varies across types of vehicles. The relationship is strongest in the amendment model, where each additional amendment sponsored leads to .758 more amendments being passed. This confirms the finding in Chapter 3 that amendment activity in the states is driven by a need to seal the deal. Amendments are proposed when they are likely to enhance the chance of a bill passing, rather than for position-taking. Activity is less strongly related to success in the other two models, but the relationship is still significant. Still, it would take approximately five lead sponsored bills to pass one more of these, and approximately 20 more co-sponsored bills to pass an additional one of these.

In looking at the individual level variables, some of these have effects that are similar to what was found in the sponsorship models in Chapter 3, but there are important differences. For instance, in Chapter 3, party leader status was positively related to lead and amendment sponsorship, but negatively related to co-sponsorship. However, party leader status is positively related to all types of legislative success. Interestingly, the effect is most pronounced for co-sponsorship levels; obtaining co-sponsorship from a party leader appears to be an important signal for the ultimate fate of a bill. Thus, it appears that the demands of party leadership, in terms of time, cause party leaders to co-sponsor fewer bills. Time devoted to managing the business of the legislature has to come from somewhere, and that somewhere is co-sponsorship. So when they do sign on to a bill, this serves as an indicator of its importance, enhancing leaders' success in this role.

In Chapter 3, committee chairs were significantly more active than their rank and file counterparts, and this analysis shows they are also more successful in passing all types of legislation. The relationship is strongest for co-sponsored bills; being a committee chair increases success rates by almost one percent, although this effect is obviously not particularly large.

Table 5.4 Modeling Legislative Effectiveness in the U.S. States

	Lead Passed	Co Passed	Amendment Passed
Individual Level Variables			
Party Leader	3.222**	5.383*	3.926***
	(.999)	(2.423)	(.871)
Committee Chair	.674***	.982*	.324^
	(.173)	(.417)	(.190)
Seniority	.004	−.006	−.005
	(.002)	(.005)	(.011)
Majority	.848	15.485**	−4.594
	(2.034)	(4.948)	(5.115)
Sex	−.008	.844	−.394*
	(.227)	(.573)	(.158)
Black	−.668*	−1.290	.184
	(.337)	(.817)	(.328)
Number Sponsored	.184***	.056***	.758***
	(.008)	(.001)	(.013)
Contextual Variables and Interactions			
Legislative Professionalism	−12.980***	−48.133*	
	(1.948)	(22.058)	
Term Limits	.255	6.195	1.807**
	(.622)	(6.746)	(.530)
Seniority*Term Limits	.139^	−.752***	.290**
	(.079)	(.193)	(.106)
Leader Tools	.710^	−.026	.086
	(.362)	(4.057)	(.310)
Leader Tools*Majority	−.045	.165	.647^
	(.224)	(.545)	(.393)
Leader Tools*Leader	−.843**	−1.389^	−1.035***
	(.310)	(.752)	(.263)
Process Limits	−1.525***	−7.043**	
	(.202)	(2.302)	
Divided Government	2.439***	7.367	−1.365**
	(.482)	(5.087)	(.775)
Divided Government* Majority	−.765^	−3.291**	.289
	(.401)	(.977)	(.810)
Majority Size	.154***	.453	−.073^
	(.038)	(.421)	(.062)

continued

Table 5.4 continued

	Lead Passed	Co Passed	Amendment Passed
Majority Size*Majority	.001	−.223**	.045
	(.027)	(.066)	(.062)
Democratic Control	−.814*	1.436	
	(.354)	(3.951)	
Black*Democratic Control	1.769**	.661	
	(.557)	(1.355)	
Sex*Democratic Control	.174	−.957	
	(.285)	(.768)	
Constant	−7.158	−5.296	3.997
−2 Log likelihood	−2441.38***	−3401.68***	−1056.99***
Level 1 N	1092	1093	552
Level 2 N	10	10	6

Note: For number passed models, the number of like types sponsored are included in the model (i.e. for lead passed, lead sponsored is included, while for amendments passed, amendments sponsored is included). * $p < .05$, ** $p < .01$, *** $p < .001$

However, this confirms previous research that this is a consistent and enduring relationship that persists across legislative institutions.

Other variables are only infrequently related to legislative effectiveness. For instance, majority party status is positively related to co-sponsorship success, but it is not significantly related to lead or amendment success. This is interesting as one of the key findings in past research is the consistent relationship of majority party status with activity and success. The effect of majority party status on co-sponsorship success is rather large though, as being a majority party member increases co-sponsorship success by over 15 percent. Of course, the analysis here and in Chapter 3 demonstrates that this relationship is conditioned by the institutional setting in which the legislating takes place, which is described below. Both gender and race are marginally significant in one model: gender is negatively related to amendment success and race is negatively related to lead sponsorship success. So, as in part research, individual level variables matter in determining legislative success. However, the important thing to note here, as in Chapter 3, is that these individual relationships are frequently conditioned by the legislative context in which they occur.[3]

So, for instance, the relationship between seniority and success rates is conditioned by the presence of term limits. This variable is not significantly related to success when term limits are not present. This is probably due to the fact that effective legislators most likely move into positions of power as they accumulate time in the institution. Thus, the most effective senior legislators become committee chairs and party leaders, while the rest are left behind. However, this is not the case in term limited institutions. In these chambers, as Table 5.5 shows, seniority is positively related to lead and amendment success, but negatively related to co-sponsorship success. In Chapter 3, this relationship was not significant for co-sponsorship, but was for the other sponsorship models. Here, it is significant in all models, as shown in Table 5.5. Importantly, the direction of the effect is not the same for all types of activity, indicating the need to look at contextual effect across all types of legislative vehicles. As in Chapter 3, these results suggest that term limits accelerate the acquisition of resources (particularly knowledge of the legislative process) that lead to legislative success. In term limited states, more senior legislators are more successful as lead and amendment sponsors, but less successful as co-sponsors. Perhaps this is because they devote less time to this activity; Chapter 3 revealed a negative and significant between seniority and co-sponsorship levels in term limited states. If more senior legislators are expected to take on more of the burden of lead and amendment sponsorship, then they have less time to devote to working to help move co-sponsored bills through the legislative process or to even sign on to them. Ultimately though, while Chapter 3 confirms previous research that suggests more advantaged legislators focus more on lead sponsorship, compared to co-sponsorship, the findings here show the effect of this for more senior legislators—they are ultimately less successful when they do engage in this activity.

The success rate of party leaders is also conditioned by the amount of legislative tools they have, as in Chapter 3. There is a negative relationship between tools and success, to the extent that leaders in institutions with the most tools, like Indiana, are slightly less successful, although the substantive effect in this chamber is small. The biggest effect is in institutions with the least tools, like Wyoming and Arkansas, where leaders are more successful. Figure 5.2 shows the predicted success rates of party leaders, given the tools

Table 5.5 Seniority Simple Slopes, Controlling for the Presence of Term Limits

	Lead Passed	Co Passed	Amendments Passed
No Limits	.004	−.006	−.005
	(.002)	(.005)	(.011)
Term Limited	.142^	−.758***	.276**
	(.079)	(.193)	(.105)

Note: * p < .05, ** p < .01, *** p < .001

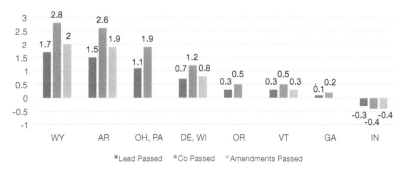

Figure 5.2 Success of Part Leaders vs. Non-Party Leaders, based on Leader Tools

available. The effect is most pronounced for co-sponsorship levels. A party leader in Indiana is predicted to pass fewer co-sponsored bills than a rank and file member, while in Wyoming, a party leader would pass close to three more co-sponsored bills. Slightly smaller effects are found for lead sponsorship, where the difference in Wyoming is approximately two bills and in Indiana it is just .3.

The relationship between majority party status and co-sponsorship success is also conditioned by a number of contextual variables; however, recalculated standard errors reveal no significant interactive relationships for lead or amendment sponsorship. Increased leader tools enhance the success of majority party members, while the presence of divided government and increased majority size in the chamber tampers this relationship, although the main effect shows that majority party members are generally more successful than their minority party counterparts. Figure 5.3 shows the predicted co-sponsorship success rates based on these findings and the actual values for these contextual variables in each state.[4] Generally speaking, in most chambers, majority party members are more successful than their minority party counterparts, but in Arkansas and Wyoming, they are slightly less successful. The effect of divided government is not particularly surprising. When the other party controls another institution in government, then having minority party members sign on becomes an important signal about the viability of a bill. The negative effect of the majority size confirms, again, the free-riding hypothesis. When the majority is so large, as it is in Arkansas (75 percent) and Wyoming (71.67 percent), there is less of an urgency to secure majority party co-sponsors as opposed to an institution like Oregon, where the margin of control is less than two percent.

In Chapter 3, black legislators were less likely to engage in lead sponsorship in Republican institution. The important conditioning effect of

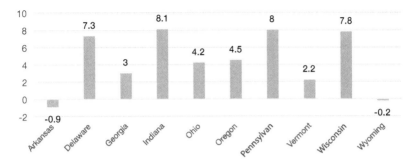

Figure 5.3 Majority Party Co-Sponsorship Success, based on Leader Tools, Divided Government, and Majority Size

control of the chamber continues in the lead success model, as Table 5.6 shows. Black legislators are less likely to secure passage of their lead sponsored bills in Republican institutions, even after controlling for the effect of majority party status. But in Democratic chambers, African American legislators are more successful, securing the passage of 3.5 more bills. As in Chapter 3, Democratic legislatures appear to be more amendable to the proposals of African American legislators, all other things being equal; that is, it reduces the costs of lead sponsorship for this group of legislators, while Republican control raises these costs.

In addition to the conditioning effects, some of the state level variables affect legislative success on their own. Both institutional rules and resources matter, as do political conditions. While some research has shown that legislative effectiveness is enhanced in more professional chambers (when comparing the number and percentage of bills passed across all states), the analysis here shows that legislative professionalism is negatively related to both lead and co-sponsor effectiveness. Legislators in Wisconsin, the most professional legislature here (.459) are predicted to pass just over five (5.22) fewer lead sponsored bills than their counterparts in the Wyoming, the least professional legislature here (.057). Similarly, legislators in Wisconsin are

Table 5.6 Race Simple Slopes, Controlling for Party Control of the Chamber

	Lead Passed
Republican	−.660^
	(.337)
Democratic	3.521**
	(1.116)

Note: * p < .05, ** p < .01, > p < .001

predicted to pass almost 20 (19.35) fewer co-sponsored bills than legislators in Wyoming. Rather than using the additional time and resources available in more professional chambers to propose and pass more legislation, it seems these legislators give more scrutiny to these measures instead, leading to lower overall effectiveness rates.[5] Furthermore, the results support the notion that position-taking, via co-sponsorship activity, is more common in more professional legislatures. Here, the additional resources associated with professionalism lead less success, due to greater scrutiny.

However, the diminished resources associated with term limits have the opposite effect, at least for amendments. Term limits are significantly related to amendment success, with legislators in term limited states pass almost two additional amendments than legislators in non-term limited states. Perhaps due to the overall inexperience of legislators in term-limited states, less negotiating gets done prior and during the legislative process, so more amendments are needed to seal the deal. In states where greater knowledge of the process and deeper relationships exists, these sort of agreements are probably worked out more informally, whereas in term limited states, amendments are needed. The disparate impact of resources on the different types of activity (term limits, which reduce resources, lead to less amendment success, but legislative professionalism, which increase resources, lead to less lead and co-sponsorship success) demonstrate the importance of examining different types of legislative activity to understand how these variables affect legislating.

Next, as in Chapter 3, process limits have a negative impact on effectiveness, both for lead and co-sponsored bills. In the lead sponsorship model, each limit leads to 1.5 fewer lead sponsored bills passing, while in the co-sponsorship model, each limit leads to seven fewer co-sponsored bills passing. These limits, then, have their intended effect, in that they reduce the number of bills going into and coming out of the legislative pipeline. As in Chapter 3, the models in Table 5.4 were re-run with individual limits substituted in placed of the summative variable; the results are shown in Table 5.7.[6] Unlike in Chapter 3, both limits and deadlines negatively affect lead sponsorship success; however, as in Chapter 3, only deadlines for bills affect co-sponsorship success. For co-sponsorship, having deadlines reduces the time to find co-sponsors, leading to less co-sponsorship overall and less success. Again, these limits reduce the material in the pipeline. While it might be reasonable to think that there were be more wheat and less chaff and hence greater success, it turns out that these limits are fairly indiscriminate in what they eliminate. Whether legislators are limited in the number of bills they can introduce or the time they have for introducing them, the end result is that they are less successful overall.

Table 5.7 Modeling the Effect of Individual Process Limits

	Lead Sponsorship	Co-Sponsorship		
Limited Introductions	−3.087*** (.666)			
Introduction Deadline	−2.695*** (.434)	−20.982*** (1.640)		
Signature Limits			−14.082 (9.109)	
Co–Sponsor Deadline				−32.164 (34.499)
−2 Log likelihood	−2437.97	−3398.08***	−3401.74**	−6771.98***
Level 1 N	1092	1093	1095	1093
Level 2 N	10	10	10	10
Level 2 N	10	10	6	

Note: p < .05, ** p < .01, *** p < .001

Finally, political conditions matter here too. Both majority size and divided government have a positive effect on lead sponsorship success and a negative effect on amendment success. As noted above, the effect of majority size is confirmation of the free-riding hypothesis. Every 10 percent increase in majority size reduces lead sponsorship success by approximately 1.5 bills. The effect of divided government is more complicated though, as divided government increases lead sponsorship success, but decreases amendment sponsorship success. Given that this variable is interacted with majority party status of the sponsor, the stand-alone variable indicates that minority party sponsors are slightly more successful under conditions of divided government. This is not altogether surprising as divided government produces incentives to work across the aisle. These legislators are less successful in securing passage of their amendments, though, pointing to the recurring theme that the work of amending bills falls to those with institutional resources (like party leaders) or bill authors. Democratic control also leads to lower levels of lead sponsorship success overall, although the effect size is small, at less than one bill.

All in all then, the results presented here conform the bottom line from Chapter 3: context matters in that it shapes the activity and effectiveness of individual legislators. Importantly, the effect of these contextual variables is not always consistent across different types of legislative vehicles. To be sure, individual resources are more likely to be positively related to legislative success, whereas their relationship to sponsorship levels are more nuanced. But this makes sense. When legislators obtain many of these resources, they also come with obligations to do more work. Therefore, they must divert their time away from certain types of activity. However, they do this with the understanding that these resources will enhance their success when they do devote time to these activities, and generally speaking, the results presented here confirm that. Finally, the political conditions and institutional rules and resources surrounding legislative institutions matter too, in that they condition the success rates of individual legislators. But these conditions do not affect all legislators and all types of activity equally, so it is important to consider them in determining who will be successful in any given chamber.

Deference to Committee Decision-Making

Of course, as Chapter 4 demonstrated, context also conditions the role of committees in the legislative process, so the next question to ask is whether these committee variables play a role in determining what happens to legislation that comes through committees. Of particular interest is the intersection between what committees want and recommend and what the chamber wants and recommends. Conventional wisdom holds that the floor of the parent chamber will defer to the reports of committees. For example, Squire and Moncrief (2010, 176) argue that "for the most part, legislators on the floor follow the recommendation of the committee report." However, Table 5.8 shows this is not true in all cases.[7] Of the close to 4,000 bills (3995) that passed committees, 12.6 percent of them were not approved by the full chamber. Furthermore, there is marked variation in the extent to which chambers are deferential to the decisions of these committees. For instance, in Vermont during the 2007–2008 session, only five of the 134 bills (out of 896 introduced in this session) received a positive report by a committee but did not pass the on the floor. However, in Georgia, 140 bills of the 694 that came out of committee never made it out of the House. In some states, such as Arkansas, Pennsylvania, and Vermont, the floor is, generally speaking, deferential to committees, as less than four percent of all bills in the session pass committee but do not pass the chamber. In Pennsylvania, only nine bills approved by committee were not passed by the floor. As noted in Chapter 4, almost all bills in Pennsylvania go through the Appropriations Committee prior to a floor vote; clearly, this committee, which is also stacked, appears to screen bills to protect party interests and so reports out very few bills not supported by the full chamber. But while chambers are generally deferential to committees in some states, it is clear this is less true in states like Delaware, Georgia, Ohio, and Wisconsin. In each of these states, more than 20 percent of the bills passed by the committee did not make it out of the house.[8]

Table 5.8: Deference to Committees

State	Passed Committee Not Floor (%)	Committee Sponsored Passed (%)
Arkansas	2.94	99
Delaware	27.44	
Georgia	20.17	
Indiana	10.05	
Ohio	20.93	
Oregon	17.36	38
Pennsylvania	2.67	
Vermont	3.73	86.8
Wisconsin	20.65	100
Wyoming	12.85	77.0

Furthermore, in those states where committees themselves can sponsors bills, there is also variation in how deferential the floor is to these proposals. As noted in Chapter 4, committees rarely serve as bill sponsors in the Wisconsin House, but when they do, the chamber is completely deferential—100 percent of these bills were passed by the House.[9] Similarly, in Arkansas, only two committee sponsored bills did not pass, whereas in Oregon, only 38 percent of these bills passed. Committee sponsored bills in Oregon are more likely to pass than other bills in that chamber, but clearly, the floor is not as deferential to these proposals here as compared to Arkansas. This may be due to institutional rules and norms about how these bills come about. In Arkansas, rules require the committee to unanimously agree to sponsor a bill; thus, committee sponsorship requires bipartisan support, which probably serves as a positive cue to the full chamber. In Oregon though, committees work on important issues during the interim between biennial sessions, and only a majority is required for the committee to sponsor bills that come from work. Thus, committee sponsorship serves as a signal, as presumably these committee members know something about an issue having studied it, but the signal is not as strong as compared to Arkansas because not all committee members have to support the bill. Thus, institutional rules influence how committee bills are received by the floor, highlighting the importance of context in shaping the legislative process.

Given the small number of states where committees serve as sponsors (and where there is actual variation in the committees that serve in this role), predicting deference to committee bills is difficult. However, there is variation in floor deference to committee reports, so the question is whether the attributes of committees and the context in which these decisions takes place shape the level of deference in these chambers.

As in Chapter 4, committee variables should be related to whether the floor is deferential to a given bill. The floor of the chamber should be more deferential to bills that are sponsored by committees as the general expectation is that standard operating procedure is to accept committee proposals. Bills that are approved by more than one committee should be more likely to pass as well; bills that have survived multiple rounds of review should be more likely to clear one last hurdle. Given that the party often seeks to empower leaders and committees so as to protect party interests, the floor should be more likely to defer to committees with more party members. The floor should also be more willing to defer to prestige committees such as Appropriations and Ways and Means, although given the latter committee deals with raising revenue, the floor may be less deferential to bills that emerge from this committee. Following from Chapter 4, larger committees report fewer bills because it is harder to forge agreement with more members, but once they have reached consensus, the floor should be more likely to respect this, leading to more deference. However, the floor should be less deferential to committees with minority party chairs simply because the majority of the members are less likely to share common interests with a minority party member.

Of course, context should matter here too. In Chapter 4, the key takeaway was that political contextual variables are of particular importance in understanding variation in committee activity. When parties have greater difficulty in controlling the process (or the cost of party control is higher), they should be more likely to use committees to help in this endeavor. Therefore, political variables, such as the margin of party control in the chamber and divided government, should interact with the margin of party control on the committee. When there is divided government and when the margin of control is larger (leading to more free-riding problems), the floor should be more deferential to these stacked committees. Legislative professionalism should lead to less deference as individual members have the resources to counter those of committees. Term limits could lead to more deference—legislators do not have as much experience, so they defer to committee decisions—or they could lead to less deference—legislators do not have the developed relationships that lead to deference. As with previous chapters, the context in which decisions are made about legislating should shape both overall deference and the relationship of committee level variables to the dependent variable, which indicates if a bill passed the entire chamber.

And indeed, the variance components model indicates that there is significant variation between the states in the rate at which these chambers pass bills reported out of committees.[10] The variance partition coefficient for this model suggests that a little over 26 percent of the variance in this model is due to factors at the state level.

Table 5.9 Modeling Floor Deference to Committee Reports

	Passed Floor
Committee Level Variables	
Lead Sponsor Committee	.297***
	(.055)
Committee Size	.005
	(.011)
Multiple Committee Referrals	−1.164***
	(.205)
Minority Party Chair	−.062
	(.442)
Majority Percent	−.911^
	(.480)
Appropriations	1.445***
	(.375)
Ways and Means	−.619**
	(.193)
Contextual Variables and Interactions	
Legislative Professionalism	−1.497
	(1.920)
Term Limits	2.966*
	(1.290)
Committee Power	1.390*
	(.550)
Divided Government	1.568*
	(1.075)
Divided * Committee Majority Percent	.464**
	(.139)
Chamber Majority Party Percent	.022
	(.029)
Chamber Majority*Committee Majority Percent	.010
	(.008)
Constant	−5.967
−2 Log likelihood	−1341.84
Level 1 N	4472
Level 2 N	10

Note: p < .05, ** p < .01, *** p < .001

Table 5.9 presents the results of a multi-level logistic regression model; the dependent variable is whether a bill that passed the committee also passed on the floor, so higher values represent a greater likelihood of a bill passing. To start, the coefficients in the Table 5.9 have a cluster-specific interpretation (Steel 2009); that is, these coefficients represent the average effects within the same state. So for instance, the lead sponsor committee variable coefficient represents the difference in the odds that a bill will be passed by the floor, comparing committee sponsored bills and other bills, in a given state. These predicted probabilities associated with these effects are reported in row one of Table 5.10 below. State specific effects are reported in the subsequent rows of Table 5.10; all of the predicted probabilities are calculated per Steele (2009).

Overall, some of the results conform to expectations, while others run counter. Given that bills are unlikely to be killed by the floor as it is, the effect sizes are generally small, but there are still some significant relationships. Having a committee serve as lead sponsor increases the likelihood of passing by just about five percent (4.9); the odds of passing increase from 76.6 percent to 81.5 percent.[11] Bills that are referred to multiple committees are less likely to be passed by the floor, despite the fact that the bill has already received support from the majority of two separate groups of legislators. The odds of a bill passing decrease to almost 50 percent when it is referred to multiple committees, contrary to expectations. This variable may serve as a proxy for the controversy surrounding a given bill, with more controversial bills receiving more scrutiny by committees and thus more scrutiny by the floor. Alternatively, party leaders may use multiple referrals as a way to increase the chance of a bill dying. Regardless of the rationale, multiple referrals serve as a cue to the floor to give greater scrutiny to a bill. Bills from the Appropriations Committees almost never die; the predicted probability of a bill from Appropriations passing is 93.3 percent, as opposed to 76.6 percent for bills from other committees. Bills from Ways and Means Committees are less likely to pass; the odds of a bill from this committee passing are just 63.8 percent. Perhaps this reflects a general aversion to bills that increase revenues.

The committee majority percentage variable is a z score, which means that bills reported out of a committee that are one standard deviation above the chamber mean for committee party balance are 6.6 percent more likely to be killed by the chamber in the average state than a bill from a non-stacked committee (odds of passing are .766 versus .700). Of course, this relationship is complicated by the fact that this variable is interacted with divided government and majority size in this model. Once standard errors are recalculated, the interaction with divided government is no longer significant, but majority size interaction is.[12] As the chamber margin increases, the

Table 5.10 Predicted Probabilities of Bill Passage

	Committee Variables at Mode	Committee Lead	Multiple Referrals	Committee Percent One Standard Deviation Above Mean	Committee Percent One Standard Deviation Below Mean	Appropriations	Ways and Means
Cluster Specific	.766	.815	.505	.700	.821	.933	.638
Arkansas	.922	.941	.787	.910	.933	.981	.865
Delaware	.951		.860	.956	.948	.988	.914
Georgia	.937		.823	.915	.953	.984	.889
Indiana	.852		.642	.860	.843	.961	.756
Ohio	.901		.750	.868	.934	.976	.839
Oregon	.860	.892	.658	.954	.901	.963	.769
Pennsylvania	.951		.859	.954	.949	.988	.913
Vermont	.826	.865	.597	.780	.864	.952	.719
Wisconsin	.851	.884	.640	.859	.942	.960	.932
Wyoming	.962	.972	.889	.955	.969	.991	.638

probability of bill from a stacked committee passing increases by .6 percent for every one percent increase in the chamber margin. Stacked committees, then, may serve as a means to combat the free-riding problems that come with increased majority size found in earlier analyses. The probability of a bill from a stacked committee dying in a chamber with divided government and a margin of party control at the average for these states is very low too, just 5.3 percent. Thus, these committee variables have different effects in different contexts; political conditions are particularly important to influencing the effect of stacked committees.

In addition to interactive effects, some of the contextual variables are significant on their own as well. Both institutional rules and resources and political conditions matter here. Term limits reduce the likelihood of a bill not passing the chamber by a fairly substantial amount. The predicted probability of a bill passing without term limits is 76.6 percent; with term limits, this increases to 98.5 percent, all other things being equal. Clearly, legislators with less experience are more deferential to the work of committees. This is unsurprising given that research has demonstrated that committee play in an important role in nearly all U.S. state legislatures. Given that legislators have less experience to draw on in term-limited states, they appear to be more deferential to their peers on committees who are policy experts.

Committee power matters too. In chambers where committees have the most power (5), the probability of a bill not passing the chamber is .156; in chambers that have the least power among the committees here (3), the probability increases to .678. When committees are empowered to act, the chamber is much more likely to defer to the decisions they make. Clearly then, rules matter. This is not altogether surprising; after all, this is why chambers pass these rules. But the actual effect of these rules has not really been studied, so it is important to demonstrate how they matter. Here, rules that empower committees lead to greater deference.

Political conditions matter as well, as is shown by the fact that divided government is statistically significant. The presence of divided government increases the likelihood of a bill passage to just over 94 percent. As this variable is interacted with the standard deviation of the party balance on the committee, this variable here captures the effect of a committee that is at the majority party balance (a Z score of 0) under divided government, so this suggests is that bills from committees that are not stacked are less likely to die under conditions of divided government. Results from Chapter 4 show that stacked committees report fewer bills out under conditions of divided government—this is the locus of party control in these political conditions. Bills that do come out should be supported by the floor, but perhaps they are less likely to pass these along for fear that the other branches will be less inclined to support them. Bills from other committees may be less tainted and therefore more likely to pass.

Of course, while the effect of these variables within a given chamber is interesting, the effects of these variables across the different states is of real interest here. Extending the model from Steele (2009), the changes in predicted probabilities were calculated for each state, using the values for state level variables for that state (so for example, the actual committee power value for each state was multiplied by the coefficient for committee power in Table 5.9), and the state level residual for each state was utilized as opposed to including simulated values for the state residual. Steele (2009) also recommends substituting zero for the state residual as an alternative method; this is how the above predicted probabilities were calculated and are presented in the first row of the table. All other variables were set to the average or mode in calculating these probabilities. Column 1 in Table 5.10 shows the predicted probabilities for these values. Columns 2 through to 7 show the predicted probabilities when the values of the committee variables that are significant in Table 5.9 are changed.

Table 5.10 shows that the magnitude of these effects varies across the states; that is, the effect depends on context. As the results above show, having a committee serve as a lead sponsor increases the probability of a bill passing the chamber although the effect is not huge.[13] For instance, a bill sponsored by a legislator in Wyoming has about a 96 percent chance of passing, whereas a bill sponsored by a committee in the same legislature has about a 97 percent chance of passing. Ultimately, the effect of having a committee as lead sponsor is small, but significant.

However, the effect of being referred to multiple committees causes a large change in probability in some states. For instance, in Oregon, bills referred to multiple committees have a predicted probability of passing of just over 65 percent, a decrease of just over 20 percent. In Pennsylvania, the effect is much smaller as it only decreases the probability of a bill dying by just over nine percent (9.2 percent). As mentioned previously, this is because most of the filtering of bills is done by one of the committees, Appropriations. Once bills come out of that committee, they seldom fail to receive approval from the full chamber. This points to the importance of chamber norms about legislative work, a topic discussed in greater detail in the next chapter.

The next two columns of Table 5.10 show the effect of moving to one standard deviation above the chamber average for the party balance on a committee and to one standard deviation below this mark. This variable is also interacted with several state level variables; the actual value for these state level variables was used in calculating the predicted probabilities. So for instance, the divided government variable was set to zero for Arkansas, but one for Delaware. Thus, these predicted probabilities include the effect of all of these measures. Because of this, the magnitude and direction of the effect of stacked committees varies from state to state. For example, in Georgia and Ohio, two states with no divided government and fairly slim margins of control in the chamber (less than 60 percent), a bill that comes out of a stacked committee is less likely to pass. However, in Wisconsin and Delaware, two states who also have slim margins of control but divided government, a bill that comes out of a stacked committee is more likely to pass. Conversely, bills from committees that are less partisan are more likely to die in some states, but less likely to die in others. These findings demonstrate the complicated effects of context. Because context is different in each state, the effect of each variable is different. Neglecting context or including only one or two of these variables may miss important effects.

Finally, the last two columns showed the predicted probability of a bill that comes from Appropriations or Ways and Means dying. For the former, bills are much more likely to pass. For instance, the likelihood of a bill from Appropriations in Pennsylvania dying is 1.2 percent. At the higher end is Vermont, where about five percent of bills from Appropriations do not move on, a probability that is still very low. Bills from Ways and Means Committees are more likely to die though; the probability of passing is fairly low in some states, like Wyoming (63.8 percent) and Vermont (71.9 percent). Bills coming from Appropriations Committees generally deal with issues that are more palatable to legislators—spending money. On the other hand, bills coming from Ways and Means Committees generally deal with a less palatable issue—raising money. Because of this, legislators give greater scrutiny and are less deferential to bills from the latter committee.

Thus, as with Chapter 4, context matters in shaping the work of committees and how the chamber receives their work. And as with earlier analysis, both political conditions and institutional rule and resources matter. Factors like term limits, committee power, and divided government all condition whether a bill that receives a positive committee report moves out of the chamber or not. The final question then is how all of these factors shape the likelihood of any given bill receiving approval from the chamber and moving on.

Bill Passage

So far, previous analyses have looked at how context shapes the activity and success of individual legislators, the actions of committees, and the reception of committee actions by the full floor. This final analysis tackles one last question—how do the characteristics of legislators, committee, and institutions influence the ultimate fate of bills. Past research has looked at how the characteristics of individual legislators serve as cues to legislators during the bill winnowing process, but this research has neglected to examine to what extent committee characteristics shape the fate of bills. This is an oversight because other research has demonstrated that committees play an important role in state legislatures. In order to examine whether committee characteristics serves as cues to legislators, this necessitates restricting the bills under analysis to those bills that have been actively considered and approved by the committee. As a result, this analysis only includes those bills that were passed out of committee. This is an important feature of the analysis to note because the variables that serve as cues to legislators in winnowing bills out of all those introduced may not be the same as those variables that serve as cues when choosing between a smaller number of bills.

In order to predict whether any given bill is approved by the full House, both sponsor variables as well as committee variables were included in a model with contextual variables. The key question here then is what types of cues are important to legislators when the final decision point in the process comes about. Sponsor and committee variables are hypothesized to serve as cues to the full chamber who do not have the time to read and learn about every bill introduced in these chambers (Krutz 2005); these cues help legislators reduce the time costs of legislating, as they still probably do not have the time to carefully consider every bill that comes out of these committees.

As with the analysis in Chapters 3 and 4 and above, contextual variables include both those measuring institutional rules and resources and those measuring political conditions; these variables are also interacted with the sponsor and committee variables. The unit of analysis here is bill; as such, sponsor and committee variables are level 1 variables. As in previous analyses, contextual variables are level 2 variables. Table 5.11 shows the results of two separate multi-level logit models predicting whether a bill that received a positive committee report passed the house. The first column includes sponsor variables that measure the characteristics of the lead sponsor(s), while the second column includes sponsor variables that measure the characteristics of all sponsors, both lead and co-sponsors.[14]

As Table 5.11 shows, committee variables appear to take on greater importance when bills pass out of committee. Just two of the legislator variables are significant in these models, party leader and black, while several committee variables, including multiple committee referrals, the committee party balance (in the lead sponsor model), and the prestige committee variables (Appropriations and Ways and Means), are significant. Additionally, as in previous chapters, context matters as several contextual variables are significant, as are several interaction variables in the lead sponsor model.[15]

Table 5.11 Modeling Bill Passage

	Lead Sponsors	All Sponsors
Bill Variables		
Party Leader	−1.584*	−1.500
	(.739)	(1.010)
Committee Chair	.027	−.282
	(.129)	(.193)
Seniority	.006	
	(.009)	
Majority	−.507	3.730
	(1.887)	(3.232)
Female	−.135	−.021
	(.161)	(.272)
Black	−.614*	−.797*
	(.295)	(.375)
Lead Sponsor Committee	2.139**	17.264
	(.811)	(628.352)
Committee Size	−.002	−.002
	(.011)	(.011)
Multiple Committee Referrals	−1.129***	−1.172***
	(.224)	(.226)
Minority Party Chair	−.074	−.143
	(.444)	(.445)
Committee Party Balance	−.842	−.708
	(.516)	(.515)
Appropriations	1.352**	1.390***
	(.387)	(.397)
Ways and Means	−.748***	−.717***
	(.197)	(.198)
Contextual Variables and Interactions		
Legislative Professionalism	1.041	.541
	(.677)	(.686)
Term Limits	4.196***	3.203**
	(1.120)	(1.054)
Term Limits*Seniority	−.192*	
	(.077)	

continued

Table 5.11 continued

	Lead Sponsors	All Sponsors
Leader Tools	.275	.435
	(.270)	(.329)
Leader Tools*Party Leader	.538*	.566
	(.243)	(.343)
Leader Tools*Majority	−.009	−.232
	(.246)	(.382)
Process Limits	.137	.030
	(.087)	(.083)
Committee Power	1.492**	1.417**
	(.445)	(.442)
Divided Government	1.475**	1.280*
	(.553)	(.572)
Divided*Sponsor Majority	.183	.594
	(.333)	(.492)
Divided * Committee Majority Percent	.460**	.426**
	(.146)	(.146)
Chamber Majority Party Percent	.008	.082*
	(.022)	(.031)
Chamber Majority*Sponsor Majority	.009	−.045
	(.008)	(.037)
Chamber Majority*Committee Majority Percent	.009	.007
	(.008)	(.008)
Democratic Control	.697***	.863***
	(.197)	(.208)
Democratic Control*Sponsor Black	.288	.741
	(.501)	(.650)
Democratic Control*Sponsor Female	.164	−.038
	(.276)	(.430)
Constant	−9.038	−11.904
−2 Log likelihood	−1240.65***	−1229.51***
Level 1 N	3877	3791
Level 2 N	10	10

Note: $p < .05$, ** $p < .01$, *** $p < .001$

Because multi-level logistic regression models are difficult to interpret, predicted probabilities are again calculated for the significant relationships and displayed in Table 5.12. The results are generally similar across the two models, so the discussion focuses here on the effects in the lead sponsorship model, although predicted probabilities are also calculated for the co-sponsorship model. As with the committee analysis, the change in predicted probabilities was calculated for each state, using the values for state level variables for that state and the state level residual for each state. The first row of the table shows predicted probabilities with a zero value for the state residual as recommended in Steel (2009). All other variables were set to the average or mode in calculating these probabilities.[16] Column 1 in Table 5.12 shows the predicted probabilities for these values. Columns 2 through to 7 show the predicted probabilities when the significant variables from Table 5.11 are changed.

Generally speaking, the effect sizes are not large, as bills that are approved by committee are likely to pass in most chambers. But as Column 1 shows, there is variation in the rate in which bills are predicted to pass each chamber, and sponsor, committee, and contextual variables all influence this passage rate. For instance, in Ohio, bills that are approved by committee pass approximately 74.6 percent of the time. Conversely, in Pennsylvania, over 97 percent of these bills are predicted to pass. Thus, context matters in determining what happens to bills after they are reported out of committee.

A few of the individual level variables are significant. In the lead sponsor model, the party leader variable is significant as is the interaction between party leader and leader tools. Because the predicted probability in Column 2 contains the effect of all of the variables in the model (including these significant relationships), the effect of being a party leader varies in different contexts, depending on the tools available to those party leaders. So for instance, in Wyoming, where party leaders have the least tools of these states, bills sponsored by party leaders are just over eight percent (8.1 percent) less likely to pass, while in Indiana, the state where party leaders have the most tools, bills sponsored by party leaders are three percent more likely to pass. This is in contrast to the individual models from earlier in the chapter, and it highlights the complicated and nuances effects of contextual variables. Party leaders in states with fewer tools are putting forward more proposals and are generally more successful, as compared to those leaders with greater tools, when comparing these bills against all bills in the pool. But when looking at just those bills that make it out of committee, party leaders with more tools are more successful. It may be that members on the floor are more deferential to leaders with more power when it comes time for a final vote-why chance a vote against a leader when it is a visible sign of opposition?

Or perhaps leaders with fewer tools do not have the power to counter-balance the powerful signals coming from committees. Regardless of the mechanism, these results demonstrate that it is important to look at context across the legislative process to understand its influence.

The black sponsor variable is also significant in the lead sponsor model, but here, the effect in all states is negative—having a black lead sponsor decreases the likelihood of passage. In Republican controlled states, the effect is rather large; having a black lead sponsor reduces the probability of a bill passing around 10 percent. In Democratic states, the effect is smaller, but still negative; here, bills sponsored by black legislators are about five percent less likely to pass. Critical mass theorists have pointed to the need to reach a certain threshold before underrepresented groups can truly influence institutions and outcomes, and these findings are echoed here. Black legislators are disadvantaged in the legislative process; they are less disadvantaged in Democratic contexts, but they are still less successful. This may be driven by the fact that African American legislators tend to be more liberal than their Democratic peers, but it may also be driven by institutional bias against black legislators.

As the interaction between term limits and seniority is significant in the lead sponsorship model, changes in the predicted probabilities based on the seniority of legislators in these chambers were calculated in the term limited states: Arkansas and Ohio. In Arkansas, the difference between a first year legislator and a legislator who has reached the peak of seniority (six years) is just over four percent, with the former being more likely to achieve passage. In Ohio, where the maximum number of years a legislator can serve is eight, that difference is just under 20 percent (19.0). It is not entirely clear why this is the case, as past research indicates that seniority is almost always associated with greater legislative effectiveness. Perhaps in these term limited states more senior legislators devote their efforts to other tasks, such as the functioning of the institution or building relationships to secure another job. Wright (2007) found lower levels of roll call participation among term-limited legislators, suggesting they spend less time on legislating than their non-term limited peers. The findings here suggest this effect may accelerate as legislators approach their end of their time in the chamber.

Numerous committee variables are significant as well, and these effects are generally consistent with the committee model from above. Bills that are referred to multiple committees are less likely to pass, as are bills reported out of Ways and Means Committees. Conversely, bills that are sponsored by committees and bills that come out of Appropriations Committees are more likely to pass. For instance, bills sponsored by committees in Wisconsin are close to 15 percent more likely to pass. Bills that come out of the

Table 5.12 Predicted Probabilities of Bill Passage

	Variables at Mode/Mean	Party Leader	Black	Lead Committee	Multiple Referrals	Appropriations	Ways and Means
Lead Sponsorship Model							
Cluster Specific	.775	.778	.687	.967	.527	.930	.620
Arkansas	.915	.866	.872	.989	.776	.976	.835
Delaware	.800	.805	.684		.564	.939	.655
Georgia	.852	.899	.757		.650	.957	.731
Indiana	.935	.965	.902		.823	.982	.872
Ohio	.746	.698	.614	.986	.487	.919	.581
Oregon	.892	.918	.841		.728	.970	.797
Pennsylvania	.974	.967	.960		.924	.993	.946
Vermont	.934	.950	.901	.992	.821	.982	.871
Wisconsin	.834	.838	.732	.977	.619	.951	.704
Wyoming	.878	.797	.795	.984	.699	.965	.772
Co-Sponsorship Model							
Cluster Specific	.798		.797		.550	.941	.659
Arkansas	.961		.961		.885	.990	.924
Delaware	.808		.795		.566	.944	.673
Georgia	.848		.837		.633	.957	.731
Indiana	.935		.935		.817	.938	.876
Ohio	.804		.791		.559	.943	.667
Oregon	.899		.899		.734	.973	.813
Pennsylvania	.972		.972		.915	.993	.944
Vermont	.939		.939		.827	.984	.883
Wisconsin	.816		.804		.579	.947	.684
Wyoming	.854		.843		.644	.959	.741

Note: Column 1 represents the predicted probability when these variables are set to their mean, while the subsequent columns represent the effect of a 10% change in the significant variable

Appropriations Committee in Pennsylvania are virtually assured passage; just .7 percent do not pass the chamber. Conversely, bills that come out of the Ways and Means committee are less likely to pass. In Ohio, for example, just over 58 percent of these bills are predicted to be accepted by the full chamber. And as with the analysis above, multiple committee referrals reduce the probability of passing, although the effect size varies from chamber to chamber. In Pennsylvania, the reduction is just over five percent, while in other states, like Wisconsin and Delaware, the effect is much larger, at over 20 percent. No studies of bill passage have included measures of committee characteristics in addition to sponsor characteristics, but this is a mistake as Tables 5.11 and 5.12 show that these variables are significantly related to the likelihood of passage with sometimes considerable effects. If, as Krutz (2005) argues, legislators look for cues surrounding a given bill to ascertain, then legislators may also look for information related to the committee that reported the bill out.

Finally, Table 5.11 shows that contextual variables matter on their own too. Although it appears that political conditions matter more as more of these variables are significant, institutional resources do matter. The resources that matter here are those that are associated with committees; the likelihood of passage increases in chambers where committees have more powers. Using the cluster specific values, the predicted probability of passage in a chamber where committees have four powers (which is just below the average across the states), is 68.7 percent; at the highest level of committee powers among these states and on this scale (5), the predicted probability of passage is 90.7 percent, an increase of over 20 percent. Of course, this is why institutions pass rules to empower committees—to enhance their role in the process. And this analysis shows these rules have their intended effect; chambers are more deferential to committees when they have more powers.

Political conditions matter too. Divided government increases the probability of passage by about 17 percent; it appears that legislators and committees work harder under conditions of divided government to secure the approval needed to get a majority on board. Term limits also increase the probability of passage by close to 21 percent. This runs counter to Cain and Kousser's (2004) findings in Washington, where term limits led to lower passage rates. In other states, legislators may not have the knowledge or expertise to counter the decisions of their peers, so they may be more likely to go along. This may also reflect an outsized influence for Arkansas, one of just two states that have term limits here and a state with unusually high passage rates. Given the contrast between the findings here and those of Cain and Kousser (2002), this warrants future investigation. Finally, Democratic control of the chamber increases in the probability of passing by just over 14 percent, perhaps due to the more activist agendas of the party generally.

Conclusion

Of course, after these bills pass the House, there are still more hurdles to clear. Bills must also pass the Senate and be signed into law by the governor in most U.S. states. Unsurprisingly, there is also variation in the rate at these bills clear these hurdles. For instance, virtually all bills that cleared the House in Arkansas were passed by the Senate, but almost one-third of the bills that passed the House in Ohio failed to clear the Senate. Political conditions and institutional rules and resources probably help explain why there is variation in whether the upper chamber approves bills from the lower chamber, but the small number of states under examination here precludes a more thorough analysis of how and why these variables matter. This is certainly worth exploring in future analyses though, as this analysis has clearly demonstrated that context is important to understanding variations in the legislative process. Generally speaking though, when these bills are approved by both chambers, they ultimately become law as vetoes are rare. During this session, there were just 16 vetoes, across all ten states here.

Regardless of what happens after a bill clears the House, all of the findings here confirm what was found in the previous chapters: context matters. Both institutional rules and resources and political conditions shape who is more successful at legislating, how deferential chambers are to committees, and ultimately whether a given bill is likely to pass. These contextual variables affect the legislative process directly and shape the actions of legislators, party leaders, and committees by raising or lowering the costs of legislative activity. The effects may not necessarily be consistent across different types of legislative vehicles—a resource that makes one type of activity less costly may make another type of activity less costly. And the size and direction of effects varies by context too. These differences in findings when looking at all bills and just those bills that have been approved by committee also highlights the need to examine the entire legislative process. What matters at one step may not matter or may matter differently at another step in the process.

Thus, it is important to consider the institution in which legislating takes place when examining that activity. Ultimately then, the last issue is what this all means for legislatures and legislating. The next chapter looks at this question by synthesizing the findings from previous chapters and also examining what these findings mean for institutional design and practical politics.

Notes

1 There is some debate over the whether the percentage of bills or the number of bills passed is the most appropriate measure of legislative effectiveness.

The problem with a percentage is that an inactive legislator can receive the same or a better score as an active legislator, even though their patterns of effectiveness are vastly different. For instance, one legislator could sponsor and pass one bill and achieve a perfect effectiveness score, while another legislator could propose ten bills, but only manage to secure passage for eight of them. The latter legislator would appear less effective if a percentage is used even though s/he passed more bills. Both measures have been used in studies of legislative effectiveness (see for example Volden and Wiseman 2007 for percent and Cox and Terry 2008 for total number of bills). Both measures are used in the descriptive analysis, but for the reasons described above, the total number of bills passed will be used in the multivariate analysis, with controls for the number of instructions. Of course, neither of these measures registers the importance of the bills under consideration. But an analysis of the content and the scope of the bills here is not possible as there are over 12,000 bills in this dataset.

2 Given these similarities, the models here are the same as for those in Chapter 3 with two exceptions. First, in the Chapter 3 co-sponsorship models, a Pennsylvania dummy was included because co-sponsorship levels in this state were clear outliers. However, as noted above, this is not the case with the number of co-sponsored bills passed, so this dummy is not used here. Second, each of the models includes a control for the number bills or amendments that were (co)sponsored. So, the model for passage rates of lead sponsored bills includes the number of lead sponsored bills. Otherwise, the models are the same.

3 As in Chapter 3, the standard errors for all interaction terms were recalculated. The relationships discussed here were all statistically significant based on this recalculation. Relationships not discussed here were not significant when standard errors were recalculated.

4 Figure 5.3 shows predicted effect of majority party status, calculated using the actual values for leader tools, divided government, and majority size in each state. Recalculated standard errors for these interaction variables reveal they are all significant at $p < .01$.

5 As in Chapter 3, amendment data was only available for six states, so the number of state level variables had to be reduced. While it would have been theoretically preferable to include all variables, that is not possible here. As such, the two state level variables were dropped. Process limits were dropped because none of these limits were applicable to amendment activity; they all limited main bills. Additionally, legislative professionalism was dropped as it had the weakest correlation with amendment success. In alternative specifications where other state variables were dropped, legislative professionalism was never significant, so it was omitted from the model.

6 Although Table 5.7 does not show the coefficients for the other variables in the model, the results are generally speaking remain the same. For co-sponsorship, the model for introduction deadlines leads to some additional contextual variables, namely leader tools, divided government and majority size, attaining significance. In the lead sponsorship model, the leader tools variable becomes significant, but the other variables do not change.

7 The analysis only includes bills that passed out of committee, as opposed to all bills. If all bills were included, there would really be three possible outcomes for bills: dying in committee, dying on the floor and passing out of the chamber.

This section is interested in differentiating between the latter two conditions; therefore, the first outcome (dying in committee) is omitted.

8   Throughout this section of the chapter, the term deference will be used to indicate when a bill receives a positive report from the committee, but does not pass out of the House. As such, it is important to note that this does not necessarily mean that the floor actually voted in opposition to a bill. For instance, according to the Wisconsin House clerk's office, bills sometimes receive a positive report from the committee, because committees may not indefinitely postpone bills, but then are never actually scheduled to appear on the calendar. Thus, the floor never votes on them. This does not happen frequently, but it does happen. As a result, the term deference should not be taken to only mean a negative floor vote as there are other ways a bill may die after it is positively reported out of committee.

9   Interestingly, while the House is generally deferential to these committees, the Senate is less so. All of the bills sponsored by the Legislative Revision Committee became law; according to the House clerk, these bills are primarily requested by legislative agencies to fix existing statutes. But only five of the 22 bills sponsored by the Joint Legislative Council passed the Senate. The House clerk's office indicates that this committee is very good at gathering support for their proposals in the House; they generally do not sponsor a bill unless they have enough support to get it passed. This is obviously less true in the Senate.

10 As outlined in Steele (2009), a multilevel logit model for the probability of a bill passing the floor after passing out of committee with state random effects but no explanatory variables was fitted. Steele recommends a Wald test statistic for calculating significant state effects; this test produced a value of 17.852 (with a coefficient of 1.197 and a standard error of .283), which compared with a chi-squared distribution with one degree of freedom results in a p value less than .001.

11 Predicted probabilities are calculated per Steele (2009) with level 2 residuals set to zero. These predicted probabilities are displayed in the first row of Table 5.10.

12 The coefficient for the divided government interaction is .447 with a standard error of .412; for the majority size interaction, the coefficient is .901 with a standard error of .472 (p < .10).

13 The effect of having a committee serve as lead sponsor was only calculated for those states where committees can serve as lead sponsors.

14 As noted in Chapter 3, these states have some varying rules for lead sponsorship—some list only one, while others list more than one. For states that allow more than one lead sponsor, the lead sponsor variables were calculated as the proportion of lead sponsors sharing that characteristic. So for instance, most bills have a value for Committee Chair lead sponsorship that is zero or one, but if there were two lead sponsors in a state that allows this, and only one was a committee chair, that variable would equal .5 for that bill. Ultimately, this ends up affecting a small proportion of the bills under consideration here (less than one percent). For co-sponsorship though, most bills have more than one sponsor. This is not problematic for most legislator variables here; they are simply calculated as the proportion of co-sponsors with that characteristic. So a bill with three female sponsors out of five would have a value of .6 for the female variable. Calculating seniority was less straightforward here though; there are no clear theoretical justifications for calculating it as the minimum, maximum or average.

Furthermore, while the seniority of a lead sponsor may be a more accessible cue, it is hard to imagine the seniority of the fifth sponsor on a bill might serve as strong cue. As such, this variable was omitted from the co-sponsorship model.

15 Recalculated standard errors indicate the Leader Tools and Party Leader interaction is significant (coefficient = -1.046, s.e. = 5.06, $p < .05$) as is the Term Limits and Seniority interaction (coefficient = -.185, s.e. = .077, $p < .05$). The interaction between Divided Government and the Committee Party balance is no longer significant though (coefficient = -.383, s.e. = .441).

16 Because there is an even split in terms of party control of these chambers, there is no mode here, so this variable was set to one for Democratic Party control. For the lead sponsorship model, the mode for all of the legislator variables is zero (with the obvious exception of majority party), so Column 1 represents the probability when these are all at this mode (or zero), and the subsequent columns represent the probability when these variables are at one. In the co-sponsorship model, the legislator variables are set to their mean; so for example, the average proportion of black co-sponsors on these bills is .075. Column 1 represents the predicted probability when these variables are set to their mean, while the subsequent columns represent the effect of a 10 percent change in the significant variable (so Column 3 represents the predicted probability when 17.5 percent of the co-sponsors are black).

References

Bowling, Cynthia J. and Margaret R. Ferguson. 2001. "Divided Government, Interest Representation, and Policy Differences: Competing Explanations of Gridlock in the Fifty States." *Journal of Politics* 63 (1): 182–206.

Cain, Bruce E. and Thad Kousser. 2004. *Adapting to Term Limits: Recent Experiences and New Directions.* San Francisco, CA: Public Policy Institute of California.

Cox, Gary W. and William Terry. 2008. "Legislative Productivity in the 93rd –105th Congresses." *Legislative Studies Quarterly* 33: 1–16.

Gray, Virginia and David Lowery. 1995. "Interest Representation and Democratic Gridlock." *Legislative Studies Quarterly* 20 (4): 531–552.

Hicks, William D. and Daniel A. Smith. 2009. "Do Parties Matter? Explaining Legislative Productivity in American States." Paper presented at the State of the Parties: 2008 & Beyond Conference, Akron, OH.

Krutz, Glen S. 2005. "Issues and Institutions: 'Winnowing' in the U.S. Congress." *American Journal of Political Science* 49: 313–326.

Squire, Peverill. 1998. "Membership Turnover and the Efficient Processing of Legislation." *Legislative Studies Quarterly* 32 (1): 23–32.

Steele, Fiona. 2009. "Multilevel Models for Binary Responses." Center for Multilevel Modeling. Accessed at www.bristol.ac.uk/media-library/sites/cmm/migrated/documents/7-practicals-mlwin-sample.pdf on July 20, 2015.

Volden, Craig and Alan E. Wiseman. 2007. "Legislative Effectiveness in Congress." Paper Presented at the 2007 Annual Meeting of the American Political Science Association, Chicago, IL.

6 How Context Shapes the Legislative Process and Why It Matters

The simple view of the legislative process, often held by the public and students, is that when a majority of legislators support a bill, that bill will pass. Of course, research shows that the story is more complicated than this. The majority party sometimes gets rolled. Party leaders and committee chairs are not always successful. And sometimes a majority of legislators are on record as supporting a bill, yet the bill still does not pass. For instance, there were over a dozen bills introduced in Pennsylvania in the 2007–2008 legislative session that had over 102 sponsors, which is more than half of all legislators in this chamber. About a quarter of these bills were lead sponsored by a party leader or committee chair, and they all had at least some party leaders and committee chairs as co-sponsors. Majority party members constituted the majority of co-sponsors on over half of these bills too. So many if not all of the factors that research suggests would lead to bill passage, in addition to having a majority of members signed on to sponsor the bill, were present for many of these bills A simple view of legislating would also suggest passage for all of these bills. Yet only three bill of these bills passed the Pennsylvania House.

This example illustrates the limitations of the analysis presented here and of generally relying solely on data analysis to understand the legislative process. Yes—examining the legislative process in a variety of institutions can help us better understand this process conceptually, but it can miss some of the idiosyncratic events and personalities that shape the process in these unique institutions. As Squire and Moncrief (2010, 161) note, "each legislature has some quirks or oddities that have developed over time and make its process at least a little distinctive." For instance, legislators in Pennsylvania may vote on Christmas tree bills, while legislators in Ohio who do not show up for critical votes go to the duck pond and legislators in South Dakota engage in hog-housing (Kurtz 2006). As another example, naming minority party members to chair committees is part of the institutional culture in Arkansas, a practice that is virtually unheard of in the U.S. Congress.[1]

In the research presented here, this caveat is clearly in evidence in trying to understand activity and success in the sponsorship of amendments. While party leaders and committee chairs are more generally more active and successful in sponsoring these amendments, different chambers have clearly different norms about the sponsorship of amendments. For instance, in Arkansas, the lead sponsors of bills are typically the ones to introduce amendments to bills, while in Wyoming, committee chairs handle this burden. In both of these chambers, position taking is rare, and sponsors of amendments are generally successful. As the Arkansas Parliamentarian notes about the former chamber, hostile amendments are rarely pursued, and most amendments are designed to either improve a bill or garner more support. Yet despite having amendments serve similar purposes, the norms of who undertakes this process are vastly different in these two institutions.

Furthermore, these oddities and quirks can sometimes raise fundamental questions about the nature of the variables under examination and reveal the difficulty in comparing the legislative process across multiple institutions. For example, how should bill enactments be calculated? A seemingly straightforward question until one comes across the Idaho case. Bills in Idaho must be approved for printing by a standing committee before they are introduced, but about 30 percent of the proposals received by committee were never approved for printing (Squire and Moncrief 2010, 164). These bills are typically not included in any calculation of enacted bills, thus inflating Idaho's passage rate.

As another example, the Georgia House clerk only prints the chief sponsor plus four more co-sponsors on any given bill and in the official legislative journal, although the chamber does not officially have any limits on co-sponsorship. If a legislator signs on as the sixth co-sponsor, does this count as co-sponsorship? And if so, what does it mean to be a co-sponsor of a bill if that co-sponsorship is never recorded in any official publication of a state legislature?[2] This question is not limited to the Georgia House as the Rhode Island Senate and Texas House also only list the primary sponsors and four more co-sponsors, the California Assembly does not list any names on a bill, the Texas Senate lists only the chief author, and the New Mexico Senate does not list any authors (NCSL 1996). Interestingly, the Oregon Clerk's office identified the same issue in their chamber in an interview and indicated this is a function of the drafting software they use. The software only allows for six lead sponsors, although more can be added when the bill is printed. Additionally the software lists co-sponsors alphabetically, which is apparently a cause for concern among some legislators seeking credit.

Political scientists have long noted the importance of understanding the "quirks and oddities" under the guise of understanding institutional norms, although studying and acknowledging these norms has fallen out of fashion a bit. Moncrief, Thompson and Cassie (1996, 314–315) define these norms in the state legislative setting as "rules which establish the boundaries of acceptable legislative behavior" and find that there are norms in state legislatures relating to specialization, courtesy, reciprocity, institutional loyalty, and apprenticeship. Past research has verified the existence and importance of these norms in state legislatures (Herbert and McLemore 1973; Huitt 1957; Kirkpatrick 1978; Matthews 1960; Moncrief, Thompson and Cassie 1996; Wahlke et al. 1962; White 1957). For instance, Wahlke et al. (1962) identified 42 informal rules in state legislatures. Of course, the presence and importance of these norms varies from state to state, with some states placing a good deal of emphasis on these unwritten rules, while other states accept very few of them (Bernick and Wiggins 1983; Wahlke et al. 1962). One of the key things to note here, too, is the fact that these rules are generally speaking unwritten, making it difficult to systemically catalog them and research their impact.

To be sure, the states under examination here certainly have their share of norms, as noted above and throughout this book. As another example, the rules in the Wisconsin House allow committees to sponsor bills, but as the Clerk's office indicates, committees just traditionally do not sponsor bills, and "it's always been that way." So even when rules empower certain actions, norms may preclude these actions. Or vice versa.

Despite the fact that institutional norms and "quirks and oddities" matter, it is important not to overstate the case here and suggest that generalizations about the legislative process are not possible. The analysis in this book demonstrates that political conditions and rules and resources do matter in systematic ways by raising or lowering the costs of legislative activity. Variations in these contextual conditions can have important effects on the activities and outputs of legislatures. For instance, institutional rules determine who can act as sponsors, as noted in Chapter 4. In some chambers, committees can act as sponsors, while in others they cannot. But Oregon's rules are even more expansive as they allow sponsors from outside the chamber. The Governor, the Attorney General, the Commissioner of the Bureau of Labor and Industries, the Superintendent of Public Education, and even several former representatives acted as sponsors of bills in that chamber. Overall, these external actors sponsored more bills (246) than committees (241) did in this chamber.

Here, the most compelling example of how these external sponsors can influence the outputs of the legislature and even the body itself is the Public Commission on the Oregon Legislature, which was created in 2005 by an act of the state legislature (Minnis 2005). This act charged this group of 30 members with reviewing the legislature's procedures and resources and making recommendations to improve the functioning of said body.

According to the Oregon Clerk's office, much has come of this commission; it has been particularly influential in increasing the professionalization of the chamber. For instance, in 2015, the chamber allocated money to study how to increase staffing—should staff be allocated by party or by committee? While this work continues, perhaps the strongest example of the influence of this Commission is that in 2010 the legislature proposed and then the voters approved an amendment to the state constitution that allowed the legislature to move from biennial to annual legislative sessions. As the Clerk's office notes, this change in rules, which provided more resources (time) to the chamber, has led to a profound shift in the culture and norms of the institution and continues to have a lasting impact.

This also demonstrates that despite the fact that legislative rules tend to be fairly stable, they do change, and as this book demonstrates, this matters. For instance, in the 2010 session, the Arkansas Legislature adopted a new rule that imposed deadlines for the introduction of bills. Sometimes the rules change because of changing personnel. A new rule about written permission for sponsorship in Oregon, for instance, came at the recommendation of a new Clerk of the House. Other times, new rules are adopted because specific events demonstrate the need for these rules. For instance, according to the Wisconsin Clerk's office, after the 61-hour debate over Act 10, which focused on the right to collectively bargain, the Wisconsin House adopted new rules that required an MOU between the chair of the rules committee and the minority party leader to establish the rules for debate. Of course, a 24-hour debate over right to work legislation in 2015 demonstrates that institutions and the actors in them do not always follow institutional rules as they are written.

Clearly then, there is a reciprocal relationship between rules and norms, and it is important to keep an eye on both. Rules can beget norms, but norms can also beget rules. For instance, historically in Oregon, anyone could sign on as a chief sponsor to a bill. The Oregon House allows multiple "chief sponsors," although the first chief sponsor was widely regarded as the primary sponsor of a bill. There was a norm (that most legislators followed) that you had to ask the primary sponsor to sign on as an additional chief sponsor or co-sponsor, but this was not required. So in this chamber, legislators typically controlled who signed on to their bills, but not always. The only mechanism of control was an institutional norm, which worked mostly but not perfectly. However, staring in the 2015 session and as described above, there is a new rule in this chamber that requires written permission of the first chief sponsor in order to sign on to a bill. In other words, the new chamber rule has increased the costs of co-sponsorship. According to the Clerk's office, co-sponsorship will now carry more meaning. Given that the new rule also increases the costs of signing on to bills, it will be interesting to see if levels of co-sponsorship decline in this chamber. The entangled relationships between rules and norms makes it difficult (but not impossible) to study legislatures and legislating in a comparative fashion, so it is important to understand these norms and how rules are implemented in real life.

Nonetheless, it is worthwhile to study legislating in a comparative perspective, because as this book demonstrates, political conditions and rules and resources, which vary across institutional settings, matter. So with these important limitations about the difficulties of generalizing in mind, what do the findings presented here tell us about how these rules and resources shape the activity of actors in these institution and what do these findings suggest about political strategy and institutional design?

First of all, as hypothesized, the context in which legislators serve shapes their actions. Political conditions and institutional rules and resources raise or lower cost of legislating, so they shape the way legislators allocate their time. Importantly, these results presented here demonstrate these effects may not be consistent across different types of activity. For instance, seniority has a positive effect on lead sponsorship activity and success in term limited states, but a negative effect on co-sponsorship success. The amount of tools party leaders have at their disposal shapes their own behavior, in addition to the behavior of other legislators. These leaders sponsor more bills and co-sponsor fewer bills, particularly when they have few tools. Lacking institutional resources to shape the process, leaders with few tools focus their efforts on legislating to achieve party goals. Interestingly, Chapter 5 demonstrates the nuanced effect of these tools. When looking at all bills, the efforts that these party leaders put into the process appear to pay off, as they are more successful overall. But when looking at those bills that make it out of committee, leaders with more tools are better able to strong-arm their colleagues into voting for their proposals and are ultimately more successful. These tools also affect the behavior of other legislators too, altering both activity levels and success of majority party members in these chambers.

As another example, party control of the legislature not only enables the party to more easily achieve policy goals, but it also affects the behavior of individual legislators in important ways. This has important implications for groups seeking to influence the legislative process and those seeking to elect and empower groups that are underrepresented in legislatures. Typically, efforts to remedy underrepresentation focus on electing members of the underrepresented group. So for instance, there are variety of political action committees and interest groups that focus on increasing the number of black, female, and/or Hispanic legislators. Oftentimes, this is done with the belief that these legislators act differently than their legislative counterparts who belong to other groups. To be sure, this is important, and research generally confirms that legislators from these groups tend to behave differently than their peers who do not belong to these groups.

But the research presented here demonstrates that if members of these underrepresented groups are elected to environments that are not hospitable to their actions, then electing members of these groups may increase descriptive representation while having little effect on substantive representation. For instance, Chapter 3 revealed that black legislators initiate fewer bills when Republicans control the chamber; Chapter 5 demonstrated these legislators are less successful in all contexts, but this effect is even more pronounced in Republican controlled chambers. So, if the goal of groups focusing on the election of black legislators is to increase descriptive representation, then electing more black legislators in a Republican chamber may serve that aim. But if the goal of these groups is to change policy, well then, increasing the number of black representatives probably will not help as not only are black legislators less successful in these chambers, they are also less active in proposing legislation.[3]

This is hardly front-page news, but it does suggest that when the political conditions are not amenable to legislative success, rational legislators turn their attention elsewhere. For instance, Grose (2011) demonstrates that black members of Congress work more closely with their black constituents than their white counterparts. Research examining how legislators allocate their time on the job has demonstrated that black and female legislators tend to spend more time on constituency service (Richardson and Freeman 1995; Thomas 1992). This suggests that actors within these institutions react strategically to these effects. Some may react by altering how they allocate their limited time. They spend less time initiating legislation and more time co-sponsoring when they lack institutional prestige and resources, which makes sense. They may also shift away from legislating to focus on other important types of activities, such as constituency service, where their labor will bear more fruit. After all, why invest time in an activity that will probably not payoff? Conversely, legislators who have the strategic advantage will spend more time capitalizing on this advantage. As Schiller (1995, 191) argues, legislators weigh the costs and benefits of legislating and will sit on the side-lines when they do not perceive a return on their investment.

Other legislators may react by crafting legislation differently or engaging in strategic behavior in order to enhance their prospects for legislative success. For instance, one of the interviewed clerks noted that legislators in his chamber may solicit other members to serve as the lead sponsor for bills they had written in order to build support and increase the chance of success. Another noted that in a chamber where there is a gate-keeping committee, legislators wait to bring their bills forward until their ducks are in a row. These clerks also indicate that party leaders react strategically to the effects of rules and norms about the legislative process. For instance, almost all of the clerks voluntarily noted that party leaders are very careful about who they appoint as chairs to some, but not all, committees. So even though in Wisconsin there is an institutional norm that all members who are serving in at least their second term get a committee chair and in Arkansas there is a norm that some chairs will go to minority party members, party leaders know that some committees play a larger role and process more important legislation, so they think carefully in making appointments to these committees.

Of course, the fact that the rules in a given legislature have a strong effects, both direct and indirect, on how legislation is processed means that these findings have important implications for institutional design. While the term limits movement was in large part driven by concerns about the role of long-time entrenched incumbents, these legislators are no more or less successful when there are no term limits. But passing term limits serves to accelerate the process of learning by doing (Miquel and Snyder 2006) and enhance the success of more senior legislators; Chapter 5 revealed that these legislators are more successful in securing legislation they initiate (and Chapter 3 showed they initiate more legislation). So term limits have hardly shifted power away from these senior legislators. Now, to be fair, a "senior" legislator in term limited states means something different than in a non-term limited state, but given other research that suggests term limits shift power away from the legislature towards staffers and the governor and that these limits lead legislators to be less responsive to district interests (Carey, Neimi, and Powell 1998), these results suggest that these limits have not necessarily altered the balance of power in ways that proponents of term limits might have hoped.

Similarly, the National Conference of State Legislatures (NCSL 1996) notes that chambers typically pass rules that limit the number of co-sponsors or impose deadlines to reduce the number of bills in the legislative pipeline. The research presented here suggests these rules have the intended effect, although some rules have more of an impact than others. Specifically, Chapter 3 shows deadlines on introductions seem to be key in reducing initiating activity. This makes sense. If time is one of the most limited resources that legislators have, then further restricting the amount of time they have available to engage in this activity should matter. Limits on and deadlines for co-sponsors will reduce co-sponsorship levels, but not the materials in the pipeline. Interestingly, these deadlines on introductions seem to have a larger effect than even limits on introductions. Perhaps the latter are not set low enough in these chambers to have the intended effect;

perhaps in setting these limits, legislators either all set this as an aspirational goal or they engage in log-rolling—securing a favor from a legislator who has hit the cap in exchange for introducing a bill. Regardless of how this happens in these chambers, these limits are less effective in reducing legislation in the pipeline than deadlines. Thus, those favoring a reduction in the size and scope of government might want to concentrate on passing rules that impose deadlines, as opposed to rules that limit activity.

Interestingly though, increasing the amount of resources available to legislators does not necessarily have the opposite effect. Higher levels of legislative professionalism lead to fewer bills in the pipeline; it also leads to lower levels of legislative success. Extra time appears to lead to extra scrutiny for bills in the pipeline; with lower levels of legislative success, legislators appear to turn to securing a broader network of support (because legislative professionalism is positively related to co-sponsorship levels) in order to navigate this more perilous landscape. Again, this has important implications for those attempting to influence government policy as the results suggest that efforts to de-professionalize state legislatures may not have the intended effects.

Overall, the results show that institutional design matters, which has important implications both for those serving in these chambers and for those who seek to influence policy. The political conditions in any given chamber raise or lower the costs of legislating. But these effects operate differently on different individuals in these institutions; they also have different effects on different types of legislative activity. Changes in political conditions may raise the cost of one type of activity (lead sponsorship) but lower the cost of another type of activity (co-sponsorship—or vice versa). The rules and resources available to actors in these chambers matter too, again raising or lower the costs of different types of legislative behavior. In these situations, legislators respond rationally by altering their behavior. In other words, context matters.

Thus, research that examines legislative activity needs to include an examination of the context in which this activity takes place. As Squire and Hamm (2005, 1) note more than 90 percent of articles published on state legislatures and Congress focused on one institution only. Certainly, the number of multi-institution studies of legislating has increased since they published their book. But their main argument is still relevant today. As they argue (3), "truly generalizable theories should be portable from one American legislature to another. If theories prove not to be portable, at least their limitations will be illuminated in the effort." As argued earlier in this chapter, there are limits on the ability to make generalizations about the legislative process not only generally, but even just in the American context. Nonetheless, this shouldn't stop us from trying. As the analysis presented here demonstrates, decisions about how to allocate time and effort devoted to different types of legislative activity do not occur in a vacuum, so it is important to think about these contextual constraints. *Where* legislators serve shapes *how* they serve, so efforts to understand legislating and shape policy needs to take this into account.

Notes

1 As in previous chapters, all of the information in this chapter that references information from a clerk's office stems from interviews conducted with key house staff in 2015.
2 This co-sponsorship is listed on the state legislative website, so there is at least one place where this co-sponsorship is noted.
3 Of course, critical mass theory argues that it is important to elect members of underrepresented groups in order to achieve some critical mass so the institution will be more receptive to the efforts of these legislators. It is not entirely clear where the threshold for this critical mass is, but it does seem clear that women and minorities have yet to meet this critical mass in state legislatures. Regardless, the point still remains that individuals will alter their behavior based on how receptive the environment is to their efforts.

References

Carey, John M., Richard G. Niemi, and Lynda W. Powell. 1998. "Are Women State Legislators Different?" In *Women and Elective Office: Past, Present, and Future*, Sue Thomas and Clyde Wilcox (Eds.). New York: Oxford University Press.

Herbert, F. Ted and Lelan E. McLemore. 1973. "Character and Structure of Legislative Norms: Operationalizing the Norm Concept in Legislative Setting." *American Journal of Political Science* 17: 506–527.

Huitt, Ralph K. 1953. "The Morse Committee Assignment Controversy: A Study in Senate Norms." *American Political Science Review* 51: 313–329.

Kirkpatrick, Samuel A. 1978. *The Legislative Process in Oklahoma*. Norma, OK: University of Oklahoma Press.

Kurtz, Karl. 2006. "Sine Die and Other Vulgarities." Accessed at http://ncsl.type pad.com/the_thicket/2006/08/sine_die_and_ot.html on January 20, 2016.

Matthews, Donald R. 1960. *U.S. Senators and Their World*. New York: Random House.

Miquel, Gerard Padro I and James M. Snyder. 2006. "Legislative Effectiveness and Legislative Careers." *Legislative Studies Quarterly* 31: 347–381.

Minnis, Karen. 2005. "House Votes to Create Public Commission on the Legislature." Accessed at http://web.archive.org/web/20061011012422/http://www.leg.state.or.us/press_releases/minnis_speaker_071905.pdf on June 3, 2015.

Moncrief, Gary, Joel A. Thompson, and William Cassie. 1996. "Revisiting the State of U.S. State Legislative Research." *Legislative Studies Quarterly* 21: 301–335.

National Conference of State Legislatures (NCSL). 1996. Accessed at www.ncsl.org/documents/legismgt/ILP/96Tab3Pt1.pdf on October 23, 2015.

Richardson, Lillard E. Jr. and Patricia K. Freeman. 1995. "Gender Differences in Constituency Service." *Political Research Quarterly* 48: 169–179.

Schiller, Wendy J. 1995. "Senators as Political Entrepreneurs: Using Bill Sponsorship to Shape Legislative Agendas." *American Journal of Political Science* 39 (1): 186–203.

Squire, Peverill and Keith E. Hamm. 2005. *101 Chambers: Congress, State Legislatures, and the Future of Legislative Studies.* Columbus, OH: The Ohio State University Press.

Squire, Peverill and Gary Moncrief. 2010. *State Legislatures Today: Politics Under the Domes.* Boston, MA: Longman.

Thomas, Sue. 1992. "The Effects of Race and Gender on Constituency Service." *Western Political Quarterly* 45: 169–180.

Wahlke, John C., Heinz Eulau, William Buchanan, and Leroy C. Ferguson. 1962. *The Legislative System.* New York: John Wiley.

White, William S. 1957. *The Citadel: The Story of the U.S. Senate.* New York: Harper Brothers.

Index